THE NEW TEMPLE SHAKESPEARE

Edited by M. R. Ridley, M.A.

THE LIFE OF
KING HENRY VIII

by William Shakespeare

London: J. M. DENT & SONS LTD.
New York: E. P. DUTTON & CO. INC.

J. M. DENT & SONS LTD.
Aldine House · Bedford St. · London

Made in Great Britain
by
Morrison & Gibb Ltd., London and Edinburgh

First Published · · 1935
Last Reprinted · · 1948

Editor's General Note

The Text. The editor has kept before him the aim of presenting to the modern reader the nearest possible approximation to what Shakespeare actually wrote. The text is therefore conservative, and is based on the earliest reliable printed text. But to avoid distraction (*a*) the spelling is modernised, and (*b*) a limited number of universally accepted emendations is admitted without comment. Where a Quarto text exists as well as the First Folio the passages which occur only in the Quarto are enclosed in square brackets [ ] and those which occur only in the Folio in brace brackets { }.

Scene Division. The rapid continuity of the Elizabethan curtainless production is lost by the 'traditional' scene divisions. Where there is an essential difference of place these scene divisions are retained. Where on the other hand the change of place is insignificant the scene division is indicated only by a space on the page. For ease of reference, however, the 'traditional' division is retained at the head of the page and in line numbering.

Notes. Passages on which there are notes are indicated by a † in the margin.

Punctuation adheres more closely than has been usual to the 'Elizabethan' punctuation of the early texts. It is often therefore more indicative of the way in which the lines were to be delivered than of their syntactical construction.

Glossaries are arranged on a somewhat novel principle, not alphabetically, but in the order in which the words or phrases occur. The editor is much indebted to Mr J. N. Bryson for his collaboration in the preparation of the glossaries.

Preface

The Text.   The play appeared in print for the first time in the First Folio.   It is well printed, though there are some oddities of punctuation.   The stage-directions are highly elaborate.

Date of Composition.   There is a body of evidence, which need not be summarised in detail, proving that Henry VIII was a new play when it was acted at the Globe on June 29, 1613, and resulted in the theatre being burned down, owing to the thatch catching fire after the discharge of a 'peal of chambers' (presumably that in I. iv. 48).

Authorship.   There is a general, though not unanimous, agreement with Spedding's view that there are two hands to be discovered at work in the play, of which one wrote I. i., ii.; II. iii., iv.; III. ii. 1-203; V. i., and the other the rest.   On Spedding's view the first hand was Shakespeare's and the second Fletcher's. A few critics have rejected the theory of a divided authorship, and some others would either find yet a third hand or give Shakespeare's supposed share to Massinger.   But Spedding's view commands as general assent as can be expected in such a disputable question. Sir Edmund Chambers, though he 'sees no reason to dissent' from Spedding, is not wholly happy about it, and his views, as always, are worth recording.   He does not find the play very characteristic Fletcher, nor very characteristic Shakespeare either.   He finds Fletcher's touch unmistakable in I. iii and V. iv., and 'probable to possible' in the rest of the play not by Spedding attributed to Shakespeare.   But he voices the natural doubt of many readers in the quiet note 'There is some very good writing for him in the pathetic scenes, and the play as a whole is a little out of his ordinary line.' That is exactly the trouble; in a great deal of the play the accent is as certainly not Shakespeare's as it is certainly like Fletcher's; but what is being said in this familiar accent has often a firmness and a depth of feeling about it which are in Fletcher's work unhappily far from familiar. But if we deny these scenes to Fletcher, we are faced with the almost impossible task of finding another dramatist who was capable of surpassing Fletcher and yet content to imitate his manner, and in any case are venturing into a wilderness of unprofitable conjecture.

Sources. The two main sources are the inevitable Holinshed and Foxe's *Book of Martyrs*.

Duration of Action. The play covers thirteen years from 1520 (the Field of the Cloth of Gold) to 1533 (the birth and christening of Elizabeth), but it plays fast and loose with the order of events even within that period, and also inserts into it one episode, the arraignment of Cranmer, which did not occur till 1544. The time represented on the stage is seven days, with four intervals.

Criticism. *Hazlitt.*—This play contains little action or violence of passion, yet it has considerable interest of a more mild and thoughtful cast, and some of the most striking passages in the author's work. . . . Dr Johnson observes of this play, that "the meek sorrow and virtuous distress of Katherine have furnished some scenes, which may be justly numbered among the greatest efforts of tragedy. But the genius of Shakespeare comes in and goes out with Katherine. Every other part may be easily conceived and easily written." This is easily said; but with all due deference to so great a reputed authority as that of Johnson, it is not true. For instance, the scene of Buckingham led to execution is one of the most affecting and natural in Shakespeare, and one to which there is hardly an approach in any other author. Again the character of Wolsey, the description of his pride and of his fall, are inimitable, and have, besides their gorgeousness of effect, a pathos, which only the genius of Shakespear could lend to the distresses of a proud, bad man like Wolsey.

THE LIFE OF
KING HENRY VIII

DRAMATIS PERSONÆ

KING HENRY *the Eighth*.
CARDINAL WOLSEY.
CARDINAL CAMPEIUS.
CAPUCIUS, *Ambassador from the Emperor Charles V.*
CRANMER, *Archbishop of Canterbury.*
DUKE OF NORFOLK.
DUKE OF BUCKINGHAM.
DUKE OF SUFFOLK.
EARL OF SURREY.
Lord Chamberlain.
Lord Chancellor.
GARDINER, *Bishop of Winchester.*
Bishop of Lincoln.
LORD ABERGAVENNY.
LORD SANDS.

SIR HENRY GUILDFORD.	SIR THOMAS LOVELL.
SIR ANTHONY DENNY.	SIR NICHOLAS VAUX.

Secretaries to Wolsey.
CROMWELL, *Servant to Wolsey.*
GRIFFITH, *Gentleman-usher to Queen Katharine.*
Three Gentlemen.
DOCTOR BUTTS, *Physician to the King.*
Garter King-at-Arms.
Surveyor to the Duke of Buckingham.
BRANDON, and a Sergeant-at-Arms.
Door-keeper of the Council-chamber.   Porter, and his Man.
Page to Gardiner.   A Crier.

QUEEN KATHARINE, *wife to King Henry, afterwards divorced.*
ANNE BULLEN, *her Maid of Honour, afterwards Queen.*
An old Lady, friend to Anne Bullen.
PATIENCE, *woman to Queen Katharine.*

Several Lords and Ladies in the Dumb Shows ; Women attending upon the Queen ; Scribes, Officers, Guards, and other Attendants.

Spirits.

SCENE : *London ; Westminster ; Kimbolton.*

THE FAMOUS HISTORY OF THE LIFE OF
KING HENRY VIII

The Prologue

I come no more to make you laugh : things now,
That bear a weighty and a serious brow,
Sad, high, and working, full of state and woe :
Such noble scenes as draw the eye to flow
We now present.   Those that can pity, here
May (if they think it well) let fall a tear,
The subject will deserve it.   Such as give
Their money out of hope they may believe,
May here find truth too.   Those that come to see
Only a show or two, and so agree,   10
The play may pass : if they be still, and willing,
I 'll undertake may see away their shilling
Richly in two short hours.   Only they
That come to hear a merry bawdy play,
A noise of targets ; or to see a fellow
In a long motley coat, guarded with yellow,
Will be deceiv'd ; for, gentle hearers, know,
To rank our chosen truth with such a show

As fool and fight is, beside forfeiting
Our own brains, and the opinion that we bring   20
To make that only true we now intend,
Will leave us never an understanding friend.
Therefore, for goodness' sake, and as you are known
The first and happiest hearers of the town,
Be sad, as we would make ye.   Think ye see
The very persons of our noble story,   †
As they were living ; think you see them great,
And follow'd with the general throng, and sweat
Of thousand friends ; then, in a moment, see
How soon this mightiness meets misery :   30
And if you can be merry then, I 'll say
A man may weep upon his wedding-day.

Act First

SCENE I

London.   An ante-chamber in the palace

*Enter the Duke of Norfolk at one door ; at the other, the
Duke of Buckingham, and the Lord Abergavenny*

Buc. Good morrow, and well met.   How have ye done
Since last we saw in France ?

Nor.   I thank your grace ;
Healthful, and ever since a fresh admirer
Of what I saw there.
Buc.   An untimely ague
Stay'd me a prisoner in my chamber, when
Those suns of glory, those two lights of men,
Met in the vale of Andren.   †
Nor.   'Twixt Guynes and Arde,
I was then present, saw them salute on horseback,
Beheld them when they 'lighted, how they clung
In their embracement, as they grew together,   10
Which had they, what four thron'd ones could have
     weigh'd
Such a compounded one ?
Buc.   All the whole time
I was my chamber's prisoner.
Nor.   Then you lost
The view of earthly glory : men might say
Till this time pomp was single, but now married
To one above itself.   Each following day
Became the next day's master, till the last
Made former wonder its.   To-day the French,
All clinquant, all in gold, like heathen gods
Shone down the English ; and to-morrow, they   20
Made Britain India : every man that stood

3

Show'd like a mine.   Their dwarfish pages were
As cherubins, all gilt : the madams too,
Not us'd to toil, did almost sweat to bear
The pride upon them, that their very labour
Was to them as a painting : now this masque
Was cried incomparable ; and the ensuing night
Made it a fool, and beggar.   The two kings,
Equal in lustre, were now best, now worst,
As presence did present them ; him in eye   30
Still him in praise ; and being present both,
'Twas said they saw but one, and no discerner
Durst wag his tongue in censure.   When these suns
(For so they phrase 'em) by their heralds challeng'd
The noble spirits to arms, they did perform
Beyond thought's compass, that former fabulous
        story,
Being now seen possible enough, got credit,
That Bevis was believ'd.   †

Buc.   O, you go far.
Nor. As I belong to worship, and affect
In honour honesty, the tract of every thing   40
Would by a good discourser lose some life,
Which action's self was tongue to.   All was royal,
To the disposing of it nought rebell'd,
Order gave each thing view ; the office did

Distinctly his full function.

Buc.   Who did guide,   †
I mean, who set the body and the limbs
Of this great sport together, as you guess ?

Nor. One, certes, that promises no element
In such a business.

Buc.   I pray you, who, my lord ?

Nor. All this was order'd by the good discretion   50
Of the right reverend Cardinal of York.

Buc. The devil speed him ! no man's pie is freed
From his ambitious finger.   What had he
To do in these fierce vanities ?   I wonder
That such a keech can with his very bulk
Take up the rays o' the beneficial sun,
And keep it from the earth.

Nor.   Surely, sir,
There 's in him stuff that puts him to these ends ;
For, being not propp'd by ancestry, whose grace
Chalks successors their way ; nor call'd upon   60
For high feats done to the crown ; neither allied
To eminent assistants ; but, spider-like,
Out of his self-drawing web, he gives us note,
The force of his own merit makes his way
A gift that heaven gives for him, which buys
A place next to the king.

15 *b*

Abe.   I cannot tell
What heaven hath given him ; let some graver eye
Pierce into that ; but I can see his pride
Peep through each part of him : whence has he that,
If not from hell ?   The devil is a niggard,   70
Or has given all before, and he begins
A new hell in himself.

Buc.   Why the devil,
Upon this French going out, took he upon him
(Without the privity o' the king) to appoint
Who should attend on him ?   He makes up the file
Of all the gentry ; for the most part such
To whom as great a charge as little honour
He meant to lay upon : and his own letter,   †
The honourable board of council out,
Must fetch him in papers.

Abe.   I do know   80
Kinsmen of mine, three at the least, that have
By this so sicken'd their estates that never
They shall abound as formerly.

Buc.   O, many
Have broke their backs with laying manors on 'em
For this great journey.   What did this vanity   †
But minister communication of
A most poor issue ?

6

Nor.   Grievingly I think,
The peace between the French and us not values
The cost that did conclude it.

Buc.   Every man,
After the hideous storm that follow'd, was   †
A thing inspir'd, and not consulting broke   91
Into a general prophecy : That this tempest,
Dashing the garment of this peace, aboded
The sudden breach on 't.

Nor.   Which is budded out,
For France hath flaw'd the league, and hath attach'd
Our merchants' goods at Bordeaux.

Abe.   Is it therefore
The ambassador is silenc'd ?

Nor.   Marry is 't.

Abe. A proper title of a peace, and purchas'd
At a superfluous rate !

Buc.   Why, all this business
Our reverend cardinal carried.

Nor.   Like it your grace,   100
The state takes notice of the private difference
Betwixt you and the cardinal.   I advise you
(And take it from a heart that wishes towards you
Honour, and plenteous safety) that you read
The cardinal's malice and his potency

Together; to consider further that
What his high hatred would effect wants not
A minister in his power. You know his nature,
That he's revengeful; and I know his sword
Hath a sharp edge; it's long, and 't may be said   110
It reaches far, and where 'twill not extend,   †
Thither he darts it. Bosom up my counsel,
You'll find it wholesome. Lo, where comes that
    rock
That I advise your shunning.

*Enter Cardinal Wolsey, the purse borne before him, certain
of the Guard, and two Secretaries with papers. The
Cardinal in his passage fixeth his eye on Buckingham,
and Buckingham on him, both full of disdain*

Wol. The Duke of Buckingham's surveyor, ha!
    Where's his examination?

Sec.   Here, so please you.

Wol. Is he in person, ready?

Sec.   Ay, please your grace.

Wol. Well, we shall then know more, and Buckingham
    Shall lessen this big look.

                       Exeunt Wolsey and his Train

Buc. This butcher's cur is venom-mouth'd, and I   120
    Have not the power to muzzle him, therefore best
    Not wake him in his slumber. A beggar's book

Outworths a noble's blood.

Nor.   What, are you chaf'd ?
Ask God for temperance, that's the appliance only
Which your disease requires.

Buc.   I read in's looks
Matter against me, and his eye revil'd
Me as his abject object : at this instant
He bores me with some trick : he's gone to the
       king ;
I'll follow, and outstare him.

Nor.   Stay, my lord,
And let your reason with your choler question   130
What 'tis you go about : to climb steep hills
Requires slow pace at first : anger is like
A full hot horse, who being allow'd his way,
Self-mettle tires him.   Not a man in England
Can advise me like you : be to yourself
As you would to your friend.

Buc.   I'll to the king,
And from a mouth of honour quite cry down
This Ipswich fellow's insolence, or proclaim
There's difference in no persons.

Nor.   Be advis'd ;
Heat not a furnace for your foe so hot   140
That it do singe yourself : we may outrun

By violent swiftness that which we run at ;
And lose by over-running : know you not,
The fire that mounts the liquor till 't run o'er,
In seeming to augment it, wastes it ?   Be advised :
I say again there is no English soul
More stronger to direct you than yourself ;
If with the sap of reason you would quench,
Or but allay, the fire of passion.

Buc.   Sir,
I am thankful to you, and I 'll go along   150
By your prescription : but this top-proud fellow,
Whom from the flow of gall I name not, but   †
From sincere motions, by intelligence,
And proofs as clear as founts in July, when
We see each grain of gravel, I do know
To be corrupt and treasonous.

Nor.   Say not ' treasonous.'

Buc. To the king I 'll say 't, and make my vouch as strong
As shore of rock : attend.   This holy fox,
Or wolf, or both (for he is equal ravenous
As he is subtle, and as prone to mischief   160
As able to perform 't) his mind and place
Infecting one another, yea, reciprocally,
Only to show his pomp, as well in France,
As here at home, suggests the king our master

<pre>
            To this last costly treaty; the interview,
            That swallow'd so much treasure, and like a glass
            Did break i' the wrenching.
Nor.   Faith, and so it did.
Buc. Pray, give me favour, sir. This cunning cardinal
            The articles o' the combination drew
            As himself pleas'd; and they were ratified   170
            As he cried 'Thus let be,' to as much end
            As give a crutch to the dead. But our count-cardinal
            Has done this, and 'tis well; for worthy Wolsey
            (Who cannot err) he did it. Now this follows,
            (Which, as I take it, is a kind of puppy
            To the old dam, treason) Charles the emperor,   †
            Under pretence to see the queen his aunt
            (For 'twas indeed his colour, but he came
            To whisper Wolsey) here makes visitation:
            His fears were that the interview betwixt   180
            England and France might through their amity
            Breed him some prejudice; for from this league
            Peep'd harms that menac'd him: privily
            Deals with our cardinal; and, as I trow—
            Which I do well, for I am sure the emperor
            Paid ere he promis'd; whereby his suit was granted
            Ere it was ask'd—but when the way was made
            And pav'd with gold, the emperor thus desir'd,
</pre>

That he would please to alter the king's course,
And break the foresaid peace.   Let the king know   190
(As soon he shall by me) that thus the cardinal
Does buy and sell his honour as he pleases,
And for his own advantage.

Nor.   I am sorry
To hear this of him, and could wish he were
Something mistaken in 't.

Buc.   No, not a syllable :
I do pronounce him in that very shape
He shall appear in proof.

> *Enter Brandon, a Sergeant-at-arms before him, and*
> *two or three of the Guard*

Bra. Your office, sergeant ; execute it.

Ser.   Sir,
My lord the Duke of Buckingham, and Earl
Of Hereford, Stafford, and Northampton, I   200
Arrest thee of high treason, in the name
Of our most sovereign king.

Buc.   Lo you, my lord,
The net has fall'n upon me ; I shall perish
Under device and practice.

Bra.   I am sorry   †
To see you ta'en from liberty, to look on
The business present : 'tis his highness' pleasure

12

　　You shall to the Tower.

Buc.　　　　　　It will help me nothing
　　To plead mine innocence ; for that dye is on me
　　Which makes my whit'st part black.   The will of
　　　　heaven
　　Be done in this and all things !   I obey.　　　210
　　O my Lord Abergavenny, fare you well !

Bra. Nay, he must bear you company.   (*to Abergavenny*)
　　　　The king
　　Is pleas'd you shall to the Tower, till you know
　　How he determines further.

Abe.　　　　　　As the duke said,
　　The will of heaven be done, and the king's pleasure
　　By me obey'd !

Bra.　　　　Here is a warrant from
　　The king, to attach Lord Montacute ; and the bodies
　　Of the duke's confessor, John de la Car,
　　One Gilbert Peck, his chancellor,—

Buc.　　　　　　　　So, so ;
　　These are the limbs o' the plot : no more, I hope.　220

Bra. A monk o' the Chartreux.

Buc.　　　　　　O, Nicholas Hopkins ?

Bra.　　　　　　　　　　　He.

Buc. My surveyor is false ; the o'er-great cardinal
　　Hath show'd him gold ; my life is spann'd already :

13

I am the shadow of poor Buckingham,
Whose figure even this instant cloud puts on,
By darkening my clear sun.   My lords, farewell.

Exeunt

SCENE II

The same.   The council-chamber

Cornets.   Enter King Henry, leaning on the Cardinal's shoulder; the Nobles, and Sir Thomas Lovell: the Cardinal places himself under the King's feet on his right side.

Hen. My life itself, and the best heart of it,
Thanks you for this great care: I stood i' the level
Of a full-charg'd confederacy, and give thanks
To you that chok'd it.   Let be call'd before us
That gentleman of Buckingham's; in person
I 'll hear him his confessions justify,
And point by point the treasons of his master
He shall again relate.

A noise within, crying 'Room for the Queen!'   Enter Queen Katharine, ushered by the Duke of Norfolk, and the Duke of Suffolk: she kneels.   The King riseth from his state, takes her up, kisses and placeth her by him.

Kat. Nay, we must longer kneel: I am a suitor.

Hen. Arise, and take place by us : half your suit   10
     Never name to us ; you have half our power :
     The other moiety ere you ask is given,
     Repeat your will and take it.

Kat.   Thank your majesty.
     That you would love yourself, and in that love
     Not unconsider'd leave your honour, nor
     The dignity of your office, is the point
     Of my petition.

Hen.   Lady mine, proceed.

Kat. I am solicited not by a few,
     And those of true condition, that your subjects
     Are in great grievance : there have been commissions   20
     Sent down among 'em, which hath flaw'd the heart
     Of all their loyalties : wherein, although,
     My good lord cardinal, they vent reproaches
     Most bitterly on you, as putter on
     Of these exactions, yet the king, our master,
     Whose honour heaven shield from soil, even he
          escapes not
     Language unmannerly, yea, such which breaks
     The sides of loyalty, and almost appears
     In loud rebellion.

Nor.   Not 'almost' appears,
     It doth appear ; for, upon these taxations,   30

    The clothiers all, not able to maintain
    The many to them 'longing, have put off
    The spinsters, carders, fullers, weavers, who,
    Unfit for other life, compell'd by hunger
    And lack of other means, in desperate manner
    Daring the event to the teeth, are all in uproar,
    And danger serves among them.

Hen.   Taxation?
    Wherein? and what taxation? My lord cardinal,
    You that are blam'd for it alike with us,
    Know you of this taxation?

Wol.   Please you, sir,   40
    I know but of a single part in aught
    Pertains to the state, and front but in that file
    Where others tell steps with me.

Kat.   No, my lord?
    You know no more than others? But you frame
    Things that are known alike, which are not whole-
        some
    To those which would not know them, and yet must
    Perforce be their acquaintance. These exactions
    (Whereof my sovereign would have note) they are
    Most pestilent to the hearing; and, to bear 'em,
    The back is sacrifice to the load. They say   50
    They are devis'd by you, or else you suffer

Too hard an exclamation.

Hen.   Still exaction !

The nature of it ? in what kind, let 's know,
Is this exaction ?

Kat.   I am much too venturous
In tempting of your patience, but am bolden'd
Under your promis'd pardon. The subjects' grief
Comes through commissions, which compel from each
The sixth part of his substance, to be levied
Without delay ; and the pretence for this
Is nam'd, your wars in France : this makes bold mouths,
Tongues spit their duties out, and cold hearts freeze   61
Allegiance in them ; their curses now
Live where their prayers did ; and it 's come to pass,
This tractable obedience is a slave
To each incensed will. I would your highness
Would give it quick consideration ; for
There is no primer business.

Hen.   By my life,
This is against our pleasure.

Wol.   And for me,
I have no further gone in this than by
A single voice, and that not pass'd me but   70
By learned approbation of the judges. If I am

17

Traduc'd by ignorant tongues, which neither know
My faculties nor person, yet will be
The chronicles of my doing, let me say
'Tis but the fate of place, and the rough brake
That virtue must go through.   We must not stint
Our necessary actions, in the fear
To cope malicious censurers, which ever,
As ravenous fishes, do a vessel follow
That is new-trimm'd ; but benefit no further   80
Than vainly longing.   What we oft do best,
By sick interpreters (once weak ones) is
Not ours, or not allow'd ; what worst, as oft,
Hitting a grosser quality, is cried up
For our best act.   If we shall stand still,
In fear our notion will be mock'd, or carp'd at,
We should take root here, where we sit, or sit
State-statues only.

Hen.   Things done well,
And with a care, exempt themselves from fear ;
Things done without example, in their issue   90
Are to be fear'd.   Have you a precedent
Of this commission ?   I believe, not any.
We must not rend our subjects from our laws,
And stick them in our will.   Sixth part of each ?
A trembling contribution !   Why, we take

From every tree lop, bark, and part o' the timber ;
And though we leave it with a root, thus hack'd,
The air will drink the sap.   To every county
Where this is question'd send our letters, with
Free pardon to each man that has denied   100
The force of this commission : pray, look to 't ;
I put it to your care.

Wol.   (*to the Secretary*) A word with you.
Let there be letters writ to every shire,
Of the king's grace and pardon.   The griev'd commons
Hardly conceive of me : let it be nois'd
That through our intercession this revokement
And pardon comes ; I shall anon advise you
Further in the proceeding.   *Exit Secretary*

     Enter Surveyor

Kat. I am sorry that the Duke of Buckingham
Is run in your displeasure.

Hen.   It grieves many :   110
The gentleman is learn'd, and a most rare speaker ;
To nature none more bound ; his training such
That he may furnish and instruct great teachers,
And never seek for aid out of himself.   Yet see,
When these so noble benefits shall prove
Not well dispos'd, the mind growing once corrupt,

They turn to vicious forms, ten times more ugly
Than ever they were fair.   This man so complete,
Who was enroll'd 'mongst wonders, and when we,
Almost with ravish'd listening, could not find   †
His hour of speech a minute ; he, my lady,   121
Hath into monstrous habits put the graces
That once were his, and is become as black
As if besmear'd in hell.   Sit by us, you shall hear
(This was his gentleman in trust) of him
Things to strike honour sad.   Bid him recount
The fore-recited practices, whereof
We cannot feel too little, hear too much.

Wol. Stand forth, and with bold spirit relate what you,
Most like a careful subject, have collected   130
Out of the Duke of Buckingham.

Hen.   Speak freely.

Surv. First, it was usual with him (every day
It would infect his speech) that if the king
Should without issue die, he 'll carry it so
To make the sceptre his : these very words
I 've heard him utter to his son-in-law,
Lord Abergavenny, to whom by oath he menac'd
Revenge upon the cardinal.

Wol.   Please your highness note
This dangerous conception in this point,

Not friended by his wish to your high person ;   140
His will is most malignant, and it stretches
Beyond you to your friends.

Kat.   My learn'd lord cardinal,
Deliver all with charity.

Hen.   Speak on :
How grounded he his title to the crown
Upon our fail ? to this point hast thou heard him
At any time speak aught ?

Surv.   He was brought to this
By a vain prophecy of Nicholas Henton.

Hen. What was that Henton ?   †

Surv.   Sir, a Chartreux friar,
His confessor, who fed him every minute
With words of sovereignty.

Hen.   How know'st thou this ? 150

Surv. Not long before your highness sped to France,
The duke being at the Rose, within the parish
Saint Lawrence Poultney, did of me demand
What was the speech among the Londoners,
Concerning the French journey.   I replied,
Men fear'd the French would prove perfidious,
To the king's danger : presently, the duke
Said, 'twas the fear indeed, and that he doubted
'Twould prove the verity of certain words

Spoke by a holy monk, ' that oft,' says he,   160
' Hath sent to me, wishing me to permit
John de la Car, my chaplain, a choice hour
To hear from him a matter of some moment :
Whom after under the confession's seal
He solemnly had sworn, that what he spoke
My chaplain to no creature living, but
To me, should utter, with demure confidence
This pausingly ensued : neither the king, nor 's heirs
(Tell you the duke) shall prosper ; bid him strive
To the love o' the commonalty : the duke   170
Shall govern England.'

Kat.   If I know you well,
You were the duke's surveyor and lost your office
On the complaint o' the tenants : take good heed
You charge not in your spleen a noble person,
And spoil your nobler soul : I say, take heed ;
Yes, heartily beseech you.

Hen.   Let him on.
Go forward.

Surv.   On my soul, I 'll speak but truth.
I told my lord the duke, by the devil's illusions
The monk might be deceiv'd, and that 'twas dangerous
To ruminate on this so far, until   180
It forg'd him some design, which, being believ'd,

It was much like to do : he answer'd 'Tush,
It can do me no damage ; ' adding further,
That, had the king in his last sickness fail'd,
The cardinal's and Sir Thomas Lovell's heads
Should have gone off.

Hen.   Ha ! what, so rank ? Ah, ha !
There 's mischief in this man ; canst thou say further ?

Surv. I can, my liege.

Hen.   Proceed.

Surv.   Being at Greenwich,
After your highness had reprov'd the duke
About Sir William Bulmer,—

Hen.   I remember   190
Of such a time : being my sworn servant,
The duke retain'd him his.   But on ; what hence ;

Surv. 'If' quoth he 'I for this had been committed,
As to the Tower I thought, I would have play'd
The part my father meant to act upon
The usurper Richard, who being at Salisbury,
Made suit to come in 's presence ; which if granted,
As he made semblance of his duty, would
Have put his knife into him.'

Hen.   A giant traitor !

Wol. Now, madam, may his highness live in freedom,   200
And this man out of prison ?

Kat.   God mend all !

Hen. There 's something more would out of thee ; what
       say'st ?

Surv. After ' the duke his father,' with the ' knife,'
       He stretch'd him, and with one hand on his dagger,
       Another spread on 's breast, mounting his eyes,
       He did discharge a horrible oath, whose tenour
       Was, were he evil us'd, he would outgo
       His father, by as much as a performance
       Does an irresolute purpose.

Hen.   There 's his period,
       To sheathe his knife in us : he is attach'd,   210
       Call him to present trial ; if he may
       Find mercy in the law, 'tis his ; if none,
       Let him not seek 't of us : by day and night
       He 's traitor to the height.   *Exeunt*

SCENE III

An antechamber in the palace

Enter the Lord Chamberlain and Lord Sands

L.C. Is 't possible the spells of France should juggle
       Men into such strange mysteries ?

San.   New customs,
       Though they be never so ridiculous,

(Nay, let 'em be unmanly) yet are follow'd.

L.C. As far as I see, all the good our English
    Have got by the late voyage is but merely
    A fit or two o' the face ; but they are shrewd ones,
    For when they hold 'em, you would swear directly
    Their very noses had been counsellors
    To Pepin or Clotharius, they keep state so.   10

San. They have all new legs, and lame ones : one would
        take it,
    That never saw 'em pace before, the spàvin
    Or springhalt reign'd among 'em.

L.C.   Death ! my lord,
    Their clothes are after such a pagan cut too,
    That, sure, they 've worn out Christendom.

Enter Sir Thomas Lovell

                    How now ?
    What news, Sir Thomas Lovell ?

Lov.   Faith, my lord,
    I hear of none but the new proclamation,
    That 's clapp'd upon the court-gate.

L.C.   What is 't for ?

Lov. The reformation of our travell'd gallants,
    That fill the court with quarrels, talk, and tailors.   20

L.C. I 'm glad 'tis there : now I would pray our monsieurs
    To think an English courtier may be wise,

      And never see the Louvre.

Lov.   They must either
      (For so run the conditions) leave those remnants
      Of fool and feather, that they got in France,
      With all their honourable points of ignorance
      Pertaining thereunto ; as fights and fireworks,
      Abusing better men than they can be
      Out of a foreign wisdom, renouncing clean
      The faith they have in tennis and tall stockings,   30
      Short blister'd breeches, and those types of travel ;
      And understand again like honest men,   †
      Or pack to their old playfellows : there, I take it,
      They may, 'cum privilegio,' wee away   †
      The lag end of their lewdness, and be laugh'd at.

San. 'Tis time to give 'em physic, their diseases
      Are grown so catching.

L.C.   What a loss our ladies
      Will have of these trim vanities !

Lov.   Ay, marry,
      There will be woe indeed, lords ; the sly whoresons
      Have got a speeding trick to lay down ladies.   40
      A French song, and a fiddle, has no fellow.

San. The devil fiddle 'em ! I am glad they are going,
      For sure there 's no converting of 'em : now
      An honest country lord as I am, beaten

A long time out of play, may bring his plain-song,
And have an hour of hearing, and, by 'r lady,
Held current music too.

L.C.   Well said, Lord Sands;
Your colt's tooth is not cast yet?

San.   No, my lord,
Nor shall not while I have a stump.

L.C.   Sir Thomas,
Whither were you a-going?

Lov.   To the cardinal's: 50
Your lordship is a guest too.

L.C.   O, 'tis true;
This night he makes a supper, and a great one,
To many lords and ladies; there will be
The beauty of this kingdom, I 'll assure you.

Lov. That churchman bears a bounteous mind indeed,
A hand as fruitful as the land that feeds us,
His dews fall every where.

L.C.   No doubt he 's noble;
He had a black mouth that said other of him.

San. He may, my lord, 'as wherewithal: in him
Sparing would show a worse sin than ill doctrine: 60
Men of his way should be most liberal,
They are set here for examples.

L.C.   True, they are so;

27

But few now give so great ones. My barge stays ;
Your lordship shall along. Come, good Sir Thomas,
We shall be late else, which I would not be,
For I was spoke to, with Sir Henry Guildford
This night to be comptrollers.

San.   I am your lordship's.

Exeunt

SCENE IV

A hall in York Place

*Hautboys. A small table under a state for the Cardinal, a
longer table for the guests. Then enter Anne Bullen and
divers other Ladies and Gentlemen as guests, at one door ;
at another door, enter Sir Henry Guildford*

Gui. Ladies, a general welcome from his grace
Salutes ye all ; this night he dedicates
To fair content, and you : none here, he hopes,
In all this noble bevy, has brought with her
One care abroad ; he would have all as merry
As, first, good company, good wine, good welcome, †
Can make good people.

*Enter Lord Chamberlain, Lord Sands, and Sir
Thomas Lovell*

O, my lord, you 're tardy:

The very thought of this fair company
Clapp'd wings to me.

L.C.   You are young, Sir Harry Guildford.

San. Sir Thomas Lovell, had the cardinal   10
But half my lay thoughts in him, some of these
Should find a running banquet, ere they rested,
I think would better please 'em : by my life,
They are a sweet society of fair ones.

Lov. O, that your lordship were but now confessor
To one or two of these !

San.   I would I were ;
They should find easy penance.

Lov.   Faith, how easy ?

San. As easy as a down-bed would afford it.

L.C. Sweet ladies, will it please you sit ?   Sir Harry,
Place you that side, I 'll take the charge of this :   20
His grace is entering.   Nay, you must not freeze,
Two women placed together makes cold weather :
My Lord Sands, you are one will keep 'em waking ;
Pray sit between these ladies.

San.   By my faith,
And thank your lordship : by your leave, sweet
     ladies,
If I chance to talk a little wild, forgive me ;
I had it from my father.

Anne.　　　　　　　　　　Was he mad, sir?

San. O, very mad, exceeding mad, in love too;
　　　But he would bite none, just as I do now,
　　　He would kiss you twenty with a breath.

　　　　　　　　　　　　　　　　Kisses her

L.C.　　　　　　　　　　Well said, my lord.　30
　　　So, now you 're fairly seated.　Gentlemen,
　　　The penance lies on you, if these fair ladies
　　　Pass away frowning.

San.　　　　　　　　For my little cure,
　　　Let me alone.

　　　Hautboys.　Enter Cardinal Wolsey, and takes his state

Wol. You 're welcome, my fair guests: that noble lady
　　　Or gentleman that is not freely merry
　　　Is not my friend.　This, to confirm my welcome,
　　　And to you all good health.　　　*Drinks*

San.　　　　　　　Your grace is noble,
　　　Let me have such a bowl may hold my thanks,
　　　And save me so much talking.

Wol.　　　　　　　My Lord Sands,　　　40
　　　I am beholding to you: cheer your neighbours:
　　　Ladies, you are not merry; gentlemen,
　　　Whose fault is this?

San.　　　　　　The red wine first must rise
　　　In their fair cheeks, my lord, then we shall have 'em

30

  Talk us to silence.

Anne.   You are a merry gamester,
  My Lord Sands,

San.   Yes, if I make my play :
  Here 's to your ladyship, and pledge it, madam ;
  For 'tis to such a thing—

Anne.   You cannot show me.

     Drum and trumpet : chambers discharged

San. I told your grace they would talk anon.

Wol.   What 's that ?

L.C. Look out there, some of ye. *Exit Servant*

Wol.   What warlike voice, 50
  And to what end is this ?   Nay, ladies, fear not ;
  By all the laws of war you 're privileged.

      Re-enter Servant

L.C. How now, what is 't ?

Ser.   A noble troop of strangers,
  For so they seem ; they 've left their barge and landed,
  And hither make, as great ambassadors
  From foreign princes.

Wol.   Good lord chamberlain,
  Go, give 'em welcome ; you can speak the French
    tongue,
  And pray receive 'em nobly, and conduct 'em
  Into our presence, where this heaven of beauty

Shall shine at full upon them.   Some attend him.   60

*Exit Chamberlain, attended.   All
rise, and tables removed*

You have now a broken banquet, but we 'll mend it.
A good digestion to you all ; and once more
I shower a welcome on ye : welcome all.

*Hautboys.   Enter the King and others as masquers, habited
like shepherds, ushered by the Lord Chamberlain.   They
pass directly before the Cardinal, and gracefully salute
him*

A noble company ! what are their pleasures ?

L.C. Because they speak no English, thus they pray'd
To tell your grace ; that, having heard by fame
Of this so noble and so fair assembly,
This night to meet here they could do no less,
(Out of the great respect they bear to beauty)
But leave their flocks, and under your fair conduct   70
Crave leave to view these ladies, and entreat
An hour of revels with 'em.

Wol.   Say, lord chamberlain,
They have done my poor house grace ; for which I
pay 'em
A thousand thanks, and pray 'em take their pleasures.

They choose.   The King chooses Anne Bullen

Hen. The fairest hand I ever touch'd !   O beauty,

Till now I never knew thee !   *Music. Dance*

Wol. My lord !

L.C.   Your grace ?

Wol.   Pray tell 'em thus much from me :
There should be one amongst 'em, by his person,
More worthy this place than myself, to whom
(If I but knew him) with my love and duty   80
I would surrender it.

L.C.   I will, my lord. *Whispers the Masquers*

Wol. What say they ?

L.C.   Such a one, they all confess,
There is indeed, which they would have your grace
Find out, and he will take it.

Wol.   Let me see then,
By all your good leaves, gentlemen ; here I 'll make
My royal choice.

Hen.   (*unmasking*) Ye have found him, cardinal :
You hold a fair assembly ; you do well, lord :
You are a churchman, or I 'll tell you, cardinal,
I should judge now unhappily.

Wol.   I am glad
Your grace is grown so pleasant.

Hen.   My lord chamberlain,   90
Prithee come hither, what fair lady 's that ?

L.C. An 't please your grace, Sir Thomas Bullen's daughter,

      The Viscount Rochford, one of her highness' women.

Hen. By heaven, she is a dainty one.   Sweetheart,

    I were unmannerly to take you out,

    And not to kiss you.   A health, gentlemen,

    Let it go round.

Wol. Sir Thomas Lovell, is the banquet ready

    I' the privy chamber?

Lov.   Yes, my lord.

Wol.   Your grace,

    I fear, with dancing is a little heated.   100

Hen. I fear too much.

Wol.   There's fresher air, my lord,

    In the next chamber.

Hen. Lead in your ladies every one.   Sweet partner,

    I must not yet forsake you.   Let's be merry,

    Good my lord cardinal : I have half a dozen healths,

    To drink to these fair ladies, and a measure

    To lead 'em once again, and then let's dream

    Who's best in favour.   Let the music knock it.

                           Exeunt with trumpets

Act Second

SCENE I

Westminster.   A street

Enter two Gentlemen, meeting

1.*G.* Whither away so fast?

2.*G.*   O, God save ye!
Even to the hall, to hear what shall become
Of the great Duke of Buckingham.

1.*G.*   I 'll save you
That labour, sir.   All 's now done, but the ceremony
Of bringing back the prisoner.

2.*G.*   Were you there?

1.*G.* Yes indeed was I.

2.*G.*   Pray speak what has happen'd.

1.*G.* You may guess quickly what.

2.*G.*   Is he found guilty?

1.*G.* Yes, truly is he, and condemn'd upon 't.

2.*G.* I am sorry for 't.

1.*G.*   So are a number more.

2.*G.* But, pray, how pass'd it?

1.*G.* I 'll tell you in a little.   The great duke

10

35

Came to the bar ; where, to his accusations
He pleaded still not guilty, and alleged
Many sharp reasons to defeat the law.
The king's attorney on the contrary
Urg'd on the examinations, proofs, confessions
Of divers witnesses, which the duke desir'd
To him brought *viva voce* to his face ;
At which appear'd against him, his surveyor,
Sir Gilbert Peck his chancellor, and John Car,   20
Confessor to him, with that devil monk,
Hopkins, that made this mischief.

2.G.   That was he
That fed him with his prophecies.

1.G.   The same ;
All these accus'd him strongly, which he fain
Would have flung from him ; but indeed he could not ;
And so his peers, upon this evidence,
Have found him guilty of high treason.   Much
He spoke, and learnedly, for life ; but all
Was either pitied in him or forgotten.   †

2.G. After all this, how did he bear himself ?   30
1.G. When he was brought again to the bar, to hear
His knell rung out, his judgement, he was stirr'd
With such an agony, he sweat extremely,
And something spoke in choler, ill and hasty :

But he fell to himself again, and sweetly,
In all the rest show'd a most noble patience.

2.G. I do not think he fears death.

1.G.   Sure he does not,
He never was so womanish ; the cause
He may a little grieve at.

2.G.   Certainly
The cardinal is the end of this.

1.G.   ’Tis likely,   40
By all conjectures : first, Kildare’s attainder ;
Then deputy of Ireland, who remov’d,
Earl Surrey was sent thither, and in haste too,
Lest he should help his father.

2.G.   That trick of state
Was a deep envious one.

1.G.   At his return,
No doubt he will requite it ; this is noted
(And generally) whoever the king favours,
The cardinal instantly will find employment,
And far enough from court too.

2.G.   All the commons
Hate him perniciously, and, o’ my conscience,   50
Wish him ten fathom deep : this duke as much
They love and dote on ; call him bounteous Buck-
        ingham,

[15] *d*

The mirror of all courtesy—

1.G.   Stay there, sir,
And see the noble ruin'd man you speak of.

Enter Buckingham from his arraignment, tipstaves before him,
the axe with the edge towards him, halberds on each side,
accompanied with Sir Thomas Lovell, Sir Nicholas Vaux,
Sir William Sands, and common people, &c.

2.G. Let 's stand close and behold him.

Buc.   All good people,
You that thus far have come to pity me,
Hear what I say, and then go home and lose me.
I have this day receiv'd a traitor's judgement,
And by that name must die : yet heaven bear witness,
And if I have a conscience, let it sink me,   60
Even as the axe falls, if I be not faithful !
The law I bear no malice for my death,
'T has done upon the premises but justice :
But those that sought it, I could wish more Christians :
Be what they will, I heartily forgive 'em :
Yet let 'em look they glory not in mischief ;
Nor build their evils on the graves of great men ;
For then, my guiltless blood must cry against 'em.
For further life in this world I ne'er hope,
Nor will I sue, although the king have mercies   70
More than I dare make faults.   You few that lov'd me,

And dare be bold to weep for Buckingham,
His noble friends and fellows ; whom to leave
Is only bitter to him, only dying :
Go with me like good angels to my end,
And, as the long divorce of steel falls on me,
Make of your prayers one sweet sacrifice,
And lift my soul to heaven.   Lead on, o' God's name.

Lov. I do beseech your grace, for charity,
If ever any malice in your heart   80
Were hid against me, now to forgive me frankly.

Buc. Sir Thomas Lovell, I as free forgive you
As I would be forgiven : I forgive all.
There cannot be those numberless offences
'Gainst me, that I cannot take peace with : no black
   envy
Shall mark my grave.   Commend me to his grace :
And if he speak of Buckingham ; pray tell him,
You met him half in heaven : my vows and prayers
Yet are the king's ; and till my soul forsake,
Shall cry for blessings on him.   May he live   90
Longer than I have time to tell his years ;
Ever belov'd and loving may his rule be ;
And when old time shall lead him to his end,
Goodness and he fill up one monument !

Lov. To the water side I must conduct your grace ;

Then give my charge up to Sir Nicholas Vaux,
Who undertakes you to your end.

Va.   Prepare there,
The duke is coming : see the barge be ready ;
And fit it with such furniture as suits
The greatness of his person.

Buc.   Nay, Sir Nicholas,   100
Let it alone ; my state now will but mock me.
When I came hither, I was lord high constable,
And Duke of Buckingham : now, poor Edward
      Bohun ;
Yet I am richer than my base accusers,
That never knew what truth meant : I now seal it ;
And with that blood will make 'em one day groan
      for 't.
My noble father, Henry of Buckingham,
Who first rais'd head against usurping Richard,
Flying for succour to his servant Banister,
Being distress'd, was by that wretch betray'd,   110
And, without trial, fell ; God's peace be with him !
Henry the Seventh succeeding, truly pitying
My father's loss, like a most royal prince,
Restor'd me to my honours ; and out of ruins
Made my name once more noble.   Now his son,
Henry the Eighth, life, honour, name and all

That made me happy, at one stroke has taken
For ever from the world.   I had my trial,
And must needs say, a noble one ; which makes me
A little happier than my wretched father :   120
Yet thus far we are one in fortunes ; both
Fell by our servants, by those men we lov'd most :
A most unnatural and faithless service !
Heaven has an end in all : yet, you that hear me,
This from a dying man receive as certain :
Where you are liberal of your loves and counsels,
Be sure you be not loose ; for those you make friends,
And give your hearts to, when they once perceive
The least rub in your fortunes, fall away
Like water from ye, never found again   130
But where they mean to sink ye.   All good people,
Pray for me, I must now forsake ye ; the last hour
Of my long weary life is come upon me :
Farewell :
And when you would say something that is sad,
Speak how I fell.   I have done ; and God forgive
    me !   *Exeunt Duke and Train*

1.*G.* O, this is full of pity ! Sir, it calls,
    I fear, too many curses on their heads
    That were the authors.

2.*G.*   If the duke be guiltless,

'Tis full of woe : yet I can give you inkling 140
Of an ensuing evil, if it fall,
Greater than this.

1.*G.*   Good angels keep it from us !
What may it be ? You do not doubt my faith, sir ?

2.*G.* This secret is so weighty, 'twill require
A strong faith to conceal it.

1.*G.*   Let me have it ;
I do not talk much.

2.*G.*   I am confident ;
You shall, sir : did you not of late days hear
A buzzing of a separation
Between the king and Katharine ?

1.*G.*   Yes, but it held not :
For when the king once heard it, out of anger 150
He sent command to the lord mayor straight
To stop the rumour, and allay those tongues
That durst disperse it.

2.*G.*   But that slander, sir,
Is found a truth now : for it grows again
Fresher than e'er it was ; and held for certain
The king will venture at it. Either the cardinal,
Or some about him near, out of malice
To the good queen, possess'd him with a scruple
That will undo her : to confirm this too,

Cardinal Campeius is arriv'd, and lately,   160
As all think, for this business.

1.G.   'Tis the cardinal;
And merely to revenge him on the emperor,
For not bestowing on him at his asking
The archbishopric of Toledo, this is purpos'd.

2.G. I think you have hit the mark; but is 't not cruel
That she should feel the smart of this?   The cardinal
Will have his will, and she must fall.

1.G.   'Tis woeful.
We are too open here to argue this;
Let 's think in private more.   *Exeunt*

SCENE II

An ante-chamber in the palace

Enter the Lord Chamberlain, reading a letter

L.C.' My lord, the horses your lordship sent for, with
all the care I had, I saw well chosen, ridden, and
furnish'd. They were young and handsome, and
of the best breed in the north. When they were
ready to set out for London, a man of my lord
cardinal's, by commission and main power took 'em
from me, with this reason: His master would be

serv'd before a subject, if not before the king;
which stopp'd our mouths, sir.'

I fear he will indeed; well, let him have them;   10
He will have all, I think.

*Enter to the Lord Chamberlain the Dukes of Norfolk
and Suffolk*

Nor. Well met, my lord chamberlain.

L.C. Good day to both your graces.

Suf. How is the king employ'd?

L.C.   I left him private,
Full of sad thoughts and troubles.

Nor.   What's the cause?

L.C. It seems the marriage with his brother's wife
Has crept too near his conscience.

Suf.   No, his conscience
Has crept too near another lady.

Nor.   'Tis so;
This is the cardinal's doing: the king-cardinal,
That blind priest, like the eldest son of fortune,   20
Turns what he list. The king will know him one
    day.

Suf. Pray God he do! he 'll never know himself else.

Nor. How holily he works in all his business,
And with what zeal! for, now he has crack'd the
    league

Between us and the emperor (the queen's great
    nephew)
He dives into the king's soul, and there scatters
Dangers, doubts, wringing of the conscience,
Fears, and despairs, and all these for his marriage.
And out of all these, to restore the king,
He counsels a divorce, a loss of her   30
That, like a jewel, has hung twenty years
About his neck, yet never lost her lustre ;
Of her that loves him with that excellence
That angels love good men with ; even of her
That, when the greatest stroke of fortune falls,
Will bless the king : and is not this course pious ?

L.C. Heaven keep me from such counsel !   'Tis most true
These news are every where ; every tongue speaks 'em,
And every true heart weeps for 't : all that dare
Look into these affairs see this main end,   40
The French king's sister.   Heaven will one day open
The king's eyes, that so long have slept upon
This bold bad man.

Suf.   And free us from his slavery.

Nor. We had need pray,
And heartily, for our deliverance ;
Or this imperious man will work us all
From princes into pages : all men's honours

Lie like one lump before him, to be fashion'd
Into what pitch he please.

Suf. For me, my lords,
I love him not, nor fear him, there's my creed : 50
As I am made without him, so I'll stand,
If the king please ; his curses and his blessings
Touch me alike ; they're breath I not believe in.
I knew him, and I know him ; so I leave him
To him that made him proud ; the pope.

Nor. Let's in ;
And with some other business put the king
From these sad thoughts, that work too much upon
    him :
My lord, you'll bear us company ?

L.C. Excuse me,
The king has sent me otherwhere : besides,
You'll find a most unfit time to disturb him : 60
Health to your lordships.

Nor. Thanks, my good lord chamberlain.

    Exit Lord Chamberlain ; and the King draws †
        the curtain and sits reading pensively

Suf. How sad he looks ! sure, he is much afflicted.
Hen. Who's there, ha ?
Nor. Pray God he be not angry.
Hen. Who's there, I say ? How dare you thrust yourselves

46

Into my private meditations?
Who am I? ha?

Nor. A gracious king, that pardons all offences
Malice ne'er meant: our breach of duty this way
Is business of estate; in which, we come
To know your royal pleasure.

Hen.   Ye are too bold: 70
Go to; I 'll make ye know your times of business
Is this an hour for temporal affairs, ha?

          Enter Wolsey and Campeius, with a commission

Who 's there? my good lord cardinal? O my
     Wolsey,
The quiet of my wounded conscience;
Thou art a cure fit for a king; (*to Cam.*) you 're
     welcome,
Most learnèd reverend sir, into our kingdom;
Use us, and it; (*to Wol.*) my good lord, have great
     care
I be not found a talker.

Wol.   Sir, you cannot;
I would your grace would give us but an hour
Of private conference.

Hen.   (*to Nor. and Suf.*) We are busy; go.   80

Nor. (*aside to Suf.*) This priest has no pride in him?

Suf.   (*aside to Nor.*) Not to speak of:

47

I would not be so sick though for his place :
But this cannot continue.

Nor.   (*aside to Suf.*) If it do,
I 'll venture one have-at-him.

Suf.   (*aside to Nor.*) I another.

                      Exeunt Norfolk and Suffolk

Wol. Your grace has given a precedent of wisdom
Above all princes, in committing freely
Your scruple to the voice of Christendom :
Who can be angry now ? what envy reach you ?
The Spaniard, tied by blood and favour to her,
Must now confess, if they have any goodness,   90
The trial just and noble.   All the clerks,
(I mean the learned ones in Christian kingdoms)
Have their free voices : Rome (the nurse of judge-
        ment)
Invited by your noble self, hath sent
One general tongue unto us, this good man,
This just and learned priest, Cardinal Campeius,
Whom once more I present unto your highness.

Hen. And once more in mine arms I bid him welcome,
And thank the holy conclave for their loves,
They have sent me such a man I would have wish'd
        for.   100

Cam. Your grace must needs deserve all strangers' loves,

You are so noble.   To your highness' hand
I tender my commission ; by whose virtue,
The court of Rome commanding, you, my lord
Cardinal of York, are join'd with me their servant
In the unpartial judging of this business.

Hen. Two equal men : the queen shall be acquainted
Forthwith for what you come.   Where 's Gardiner ?

Wol. I know your majesty has always lov'd her
So dear in heart, not to deny her that   110
A woman of less place might ask by law,
Scholars allow'd freely to argue for her.

Hen. Ay, and the best she shall have ; and my favour
To him that does best, God forbid else : Cardinal,
Prithee call Gardiner to me, my new secretary :
I find him a fit fellow.   *Exit Wolsey*

Re-enter Wolsey, with Gardiner

Wol. (*aside to Gar.*) Give me your hand : much joy and
      favour to you ;
You are the king's now.

Gar.   (*aside to Wol.*) But to be commanded
For ever by your grace, whose hand has rais'd me.

Hen. Come hither, Gardiner.   *Walks and whispers* 120

Cam. My Lord of York, was not one Doctor Pace
In this man's place before him ?

Wol.   Yes, he was.

49

Cam. Was he not held a learned man ?

Wol.   Yes, surely.

Cam. Believe me, there's an ill opinion spread then,
    Even of yourself, lord cardinal.

Wol.   How ? of me ?

Cam. They will not stick to say you envied him ;
    And fearing he would rise (he was so virtuous)
    Kept him a foreign man still, which so griev'd him,
    That he ran mad, and died.

Wol.   Heaven's peace be with him !
    That's Christian care enough : for living murmurers, 130
    There's places of rebuke.   He was a fool ;
    For he would needs be virtuous.   That good fellow,
    If I command him, follows my appointment :
    I will have none so near else.   Learn this, brother,
    We live not to be grip'd by meaner persons.

Hen. Deliver this with modesty to the queen.

                            Exit Gardiner

    The most convenient place that I can think of
    For such receipt of learning is Black-Friars :
    There ye shall meet about this weighty business.
    My Wolsey, see it furnish'd.   O, my lord,   140
    Would it not grieve an able man to leave
    So sweet a bedfellow ?   But, conscience, conscience !
    O, 'tis a tender place, and I must leave her.   *Exeunt*

SCENE III

An ante-chamber of the Queen's apartments

Enter Anne Bullen and an old Lady

Anne. Not for that neither; here's the pang that pinches.
His highness having liv'd so long with her, and she
So good a lady, that no tongue could ever
Pronounce dishonour of her; by my life,
She never knew harm-doing: O, now, after
So many courses of the sun enthroned,
Still growing in a majesty and pomp, the which
To leave a thousand-fold more bitter than
'Tis sweet at first to acquire—after this process,
To give her the avaunt! it is a pity   10
Would move a monster.

La.   Hearts of most hard temper
Melt and lament for her.

Anne.   O, God's will! much better
She ne'er had known pomp; though 't be temporal,
Yet, if that quarrel, fortune, do divorce   †
It from the bearer, 'tis a sufferance, panging
As soul and body's severing.

La.   Alas, poor lady,
She's a stranger now again.

Anne.   So much the more
    Must pity drop upon her ; verily
    I swear, 'tis better to be lowly born,
    And range with humble livers in content,   20
    Than to be perk'd up in a glistering grief,
    And wear a golden sorrow.

La.   Our content
    Is our best having.

Anne.   By my troth, and maidenhood,
    I would not be a queen.

La.   Beshrew me, I would,
    And venture maidenhood for 't, and so would you,
    For all this spice of your hypocrisy :
    You, that have so fair parts of woman on you,
    Have (too) a woman's heart, which ever yet
    Affected eminence, wealth, sovereignty ;
    Which, to say sooth, are blessings ; and which gifts   30
    (Saving your mincing) the capacity
    Of your soft cheveril conscience would receive,
    If you might please to stretch it.

Anne.   Nay, good troth.

La. Yes, troth, and troth ; you would not be a queen ?

Anne. No, not for all the riches under heaven.

La. 'Tis strange : a three-pence bow'd would hire me,
    Old as I am, to queen it : but I pray you,

What think you of a duchess ? have you limbs
To bear that load of title ?

Anne.   No, in truth.

La. Then you are weakly made : pluck off a little ;   40
I would not be a young count in your way,
For more than blushing comes to : if your back
Cannot vouchsafe this burthen, 'tis too weak
Ever to get a boy.

Anne.   How you do talk !
I swear again, I would not be a queen
For all the world.

La.   In faith, for little England
You 'ld venture an emballing : I myself
Would for Carnarvonshire, although there 'long'd
No more to the crown but that.   Lo, who comes here ?

                          Enter the Lord Chamberlain

L.C. Good morrow, ladies ; what were 't worth to know   50
The secret of your conference ?

Anne.   My good Lord,
Not your demand ; it values not your asking :
Our mistress' sorrows we were pitying.

L.C. It was a gentle business, and becoming
The action of good women ; there is hope
All will be well.

Anne.   Now I pray God, amen !

15 *e*
                          53

L.C. You bear a gentle mind, and heavenly blessings
    Follow such creatures. That you may, fair lady,
    Perceive I speak sincerely, and high note 's
    Ta'en of your many virtues, the king's majesty   60
    Commends his good opinion of you to you ; and
    Does purpose honour to you no less flowing
    Than Marchioness of Pembroke ; to which title,
    A thousand pound a year, annual support,
    Out of his grace he adds.

Anne.   I do not know
    What kind of my obedience I should tender ;
    More than my all is nothing : nor my prayers
    Are not words duly hallow'd, nor my wishes
    More worth than empty vanities ; yet prayers and
        wishes
    Are all I can return. Beseech your lordship,   70
    Vouchsafe to speak my thanks, and my obedience,
    As from a blushing handmaid, to his highness ;
    Whose health and royalty I pray for.

L.C.   Lady,
    I shall not fail to approve the fair conceit
    The king hath of you. *(aside)* I have perus'd her well,
    Beauty and honour in her are so mingled,
    That they have caught the king : and who knows yet
    But from this lady may proceed a gem

To lighten all this isle ?—I 'll to the king,
And say I spoke with you.

Anne.   My honour'd lord.   80

Exit Lord Chamberlain

La. Why, this it is ! see, see,
    I have been begging sixteen years in court,
    (Am yet a courtier beggarly) nor could
    Come pat betwixt too early and too late
    For any suit of pounds : and you (O fate !)
    A very fresh fish here—fie, fie, fie upon
    This compell'd fortune !—have your mouth fill'd up
    Before you open it.

Anne.   This is strange to me.

La. How tastes it ? is it bitter ? forty pence, no.   †
    There was a lady once ('tis an old story)   90
    That would not be a queen, that would she not
    For all the mud in Egypt : have you heard it ?

Anne. Come, you are pleasant.

La.   With your theme, I could
    O'ermount the lark.   The Marchioness of Pembroke ?
    A thousand pounds a year for pure respect ?
    No other obligation ?   By my life,
    That promises mo thousands : honour's train
    Is longer than his foreskirt ; by this time
    I know your back will bear a duchess.   Say,

Are you not stronger than you were?

Anne.   Good lady,   100
Make yourself mirth with your particular fancy,
And leave me out on 't.   Would I had no being,
If this salute my blood a jot; it faints me
To think what follows.
The queen is comfortless, and we forgetful
In our long absence: pray, do not deliver
What here you 've heard to her.

La.   What do you think me?
                                    Exeunt

SCENE IV

A hall in Black-Friars

Trumpets, sennet and cornets.   Enter two Vergers, with short silver wands; next them, two Scribes, in the habit of doctors; after them, the Archbishop of Canterbury alone; after him, the Bishops of Lincoln, Ely, Rochester, and Saint Asaph; next them, with some small distance, follows a Gentleman bearing the purse, with the great seal, and a cardinal's hat; then two Priests, bearing each a silver cross; then a Gentleman Usher bare-headed, accompanied with a Sergeant-at-arms bearing a silver mace; then two Gentlemen bearing two great silver pillars; after

*them, side by side, the two Cardinals ; two Noblemen
with the sword and mace. The King takes place under
the cloth of state ; the two Cardinals sit under him as
judges. The Queen takes place some distance from the
King. The Bishops place themselves on each side the
court, in manner of a consistory ; below them the Scribes.
The Lords sit next the Bishops. The rest of the
Attendants stand in convenient order about the stage.*

Wol. Whilst our commission from Rome is read,
　　　Let silence be commanded.

Hen. 　　　　　　　　What 's the need ?
　　　It hath already publicly been read,
　　　And on all sides the authority allow'd,
　　　You may then spare that time.

Wol. 　　　　　　　　Be 't so, proceed.

Scr. Say, Henry King of England, come into the court.

Cri. Henry King of England, &c.

Hen. Here.

Scr. Say, Katharine Queen of England, come into the
　　　court.

Cri. Katharine Queen of England, &c.　　　　　　10

　　　*The Queen makes no answer, rises out of her chair,
　　　　　goes about the court, comes to the King, and
　　　　　kneels at his feet. Then speaks*

57

Kat. Sir, I desire you do me right and justice,
  And to bestow your pity on me ; for
  I am a most poor woman, and a stranger,
  Born out of your dominions : having here
  No judge indifferent, nor no more assurance
  Of equal friendship and proceeding.   Alas, sir ;
  In what have I offended you ? what cause
  Hath my behaviour given to your displeasure,
  That thus you should proceed to put me off,   20
  And take your good grace from me ?   Heaven witness,
  I have been to you a true and humble wife,
  At all times to your will conformable ;
  Ever in fear to kindle your dislike,
  Yea, subject to your countenance ; glad, or sorry,
  As I saw it inclin'd : when was the hour
  I ever contradicted your desire ?
  Or made it not mine too ?   Or which of your friends
  Have I not strove to love, although I knew
  He were mine enemy ? what friend of mine   30
  That had to him deriv'd your anger, did I
  Continue in my liking ? nay, gave notice
  He was from thence discharg'd.   Sir, call to mind
  That I have been your wife, in this obedience,
  Upward of twenty years, and have been blest
  With many children by you.   If in the course

And process of this time you can report,
And prove it too, against mine honour, aught ;
My bond to wedlock, or my love and duty,
Against your sacred person ; in God's name   40
Turn me away ; and let the foul'st contempt
Shut door upon me, and so give me up
To the sharp'st kind of justice.   Please you, sir,
The king, your father, was reputed for
A prince most prudent, of an excellent
And unmatch'd wit and judgement : Ferdinand,
My father, king of Spain, was reckon'd one
The wisest prince that there had reign'd by many
A year before : it is not to be question'd
That they had gather'd a wise council to them   50
Of every realm, that did debate this business,
Who deem'd our marriage lawful.   Wherefore I
      humbly
Beseech you, sir, to spare me, till I may
Be by my friends in Spain advis'd ; whose counsel
I will implore.   If not, i' the name of God
Your pleasure be fulfill'd !

Wol.   You have here, lady,
      (And of your choice) these reverend fathers, men
      Of singular integrity and learning ;
      Yea, the elect o' the land, who are assembled

To plead your cause : it shall be therefore bootless   60
That longer you desire the court, as well   †
For your own quiet, as to rectify
What is unsettled in the king.

Cam.   His grace
Hath spoken well, and justly : therefore, madam,
It 's fit this royal session do proceed,
And that (without delay) their arguments
Be now produc'd, and heard.

Kat.   Lord cardinal,
To you I speak.

Wol.   Your pleasure, madam ?

Kat.   Sir,
I am about to weep ; but, thinking that
We are a queen (or long have dream'd so) certain   70
The daughter of a king, my drops of tears
I 'll turn to sparks of fire.

Wol.   Be patient yet.

Kat. I will, when you are humble ; nay, before,
Or God will punish me. I do believe
(Induc'd by potent circumstances) that
You are mine enemy, and make my challenge,
You shall not be my judge : for it is you
Have blown this coal, betwixt my lord and me ;
Which God's dew quench ! Therefore I say again,

I utterly abhor, yea, from my soul   80
Refuse you for my judge, whom, yet once more,
I hold my most malicious foe, and think not
At all a friend to truth.

Wol.   I do profess
You speak not like yourself: who ever yet
Have stood to charity, and display'd the effects
Of disposition gentle, and of wisdom,
O'ertopping woman's power.   Madam, you do me
    wrong,
I have no spleen against you, nor injustice
For you, or any: how far I have proceeded,
Or how far further shall, is warranted   90
By a commission from the consistory,
Yea, the whole consistory of Rome.   You charge me,
That I have blown this coal: I do deny it:
The king is present: if it be known to him,
That I gainsay my deed, how may he wound,
And worthily, my falsehood, yea, as much
As you have done my truth.   If he know
That I am free of your report, he knows
I am not of your wrong.   Therefore in him
It lies to cure me, and the cure is to   100
Remove these thoughts from you: the which before
His highness shall speak in, I do beseech

You, gracious madam, to unthink your speaking,
And to say so no more.

Kat.   My lord, my lord,
I am a simple woman, much too weak
To oppose your cunning.   You 're meek, and humble-
          mouth'd ;
You sign your place, and calling, in full seeming,
With meekness and humility ; but your heart
Is cramm'd with arrogancy, spleen, and pride.
You have, by fortune, and his highness' favours,   110
Gone slightly o'er low steps, and now are mounted
Where powers are your retainers, and your words
(Domestics to you) serve your will, as 't please
Yourself pronounce their office.   I must tell you,
You tender more your person's honour than
Your high profession spiritual ; that again
I do refuse you for my judge, and here,
Before you all, appeal unto the pope,
To bring my whole cause 'fore his holiness,
And to be judg'd by him.

                    She curtsies to the King, and offers to depart

Cam.   The queen is obstinate,   120
Stubborn to justice, apt to accuse it, and
Disdainful to be tried by 't : 'tis not well.
She 's going away.

Hen. Call her again.

Cri. Katharine Queen of England, come into the court.

Gent. Ush. Madam, you are call'd back.

Kat. What need you note it? pray you, keep your way:
When you are call'd, return.   Now the Lord help!
They vex me past my patience, pray you pass on;
I will not tarry; no, nor ever more   130
Upon this business my appearance make,
In any of their courts.

       Exeunt Queen, and her Attendants

Hen.   Go thy ways, Kate;
That man i' the world who shall report he has
A better wife, let him in nought be trusted,
For speaking false in that; thou art alone
(If thy rare qualities, sweet gentleness,
Thy meekness saint-like, wife-like government,
Obeying in commanding, and thy parts
Sovereign and pious else, could speak thee out)
The queen of earthly queens.   She's noble born;   140
And like her true nobility she has
Carried herself towards me.

Wol.   Most gracious sir,
In humblest manner I require your highness,
That it shall please you to declare in hearing
Of all these ears (for where I am robb'd and bound,

There must I be unloos'd, although not there
At once and fully satisfied) whether ever I
Did broach this business to your highness, or
Laid any scruple in your way which might
Induce you to the question on 't : or ever   150
Have to you, but with thanks to God for such
A royal lady, spake one the least word that might
Be to the prejudice of her present state
Or touch of her good person ?

Hen.   My lord cardinal,
I do excuse you ; yea, upon mine honour,
I free you from 't.   You are not to be taught
That you have many enemies, that know not
Why they are so ; but like to village curs,
Bark when their fellows do.   By some of these
The queen is put in anger ; you 're excused :   160
But will you be more justified ? you ever
Have wish'd the sleeping of this business, never desir'd
It to be stirr'd ; but oft have hinder'd, oft,
The passages made toward it ; on my honour,
I speak my good lord cardinal to this point ;
And thus far clear him.   Now, what mov'd me to 't,
I will be bold with time and your attention :
Then mark the inducement.   Thus it came ; give
     heed to 't :

My conscience first receiv'd a tenderness,
Scruple, and prick, on certain speeches utter'd   170
By the Bishop of Bayonne, then French ambassador,
Who had been hither sent on the debating
A marriage 'twixt the Duke of Orleans and
Our daughter Mary : i' the progress of this business,
Ere a determinate resolution, he
(I mean the bishop) did require a respite,
Wherein he might the king his lord advertise
Whether our daughter were legitimate,
Respecting this our marriage with the dowager,
Sometimes our brother's wife.   This respite shook   180
The bosom of my conscience, enter'd me,
Yea, with a splitting power, and made to tremble
The region of my breast which forc'd such way
That many maz'd considerings did throng
And press'd in with this caution.   First, methought
I stood not in the smile of heaven, who had
Commanded nature that my lady's womb,
If it conceiv'd a male-child by me, should
Do no more offices of life to 't than
The grave does to the dead ; for her male issue   190
Or died where they were made, or shortly after
This world had air'd them : hence I took a
      thought,

65

This was a judgement on me, that my kingdom
(Well worthy the best heir o' the world) should **not**
Be gladded in 't by me : then follows that
I weigh'd the danger which my realms stood in
By this my issue's fail, and that gave to me
Many a groaning throe.   Thus hulling in
The wild sea of my conscience, I did steer
Toward this remedy, whereupon we are   200
Now present here together ; that 's to say,
I meant to rectify my conscience, which
I then did feel full sick, and yet not well,
By all the reverend fathers of the land,
And doctors learn'd.   First I began in private,
With you my Lord of Lincoln ; you remember
How under my oppression I did reek,
When I first mov'd you.

Bis.   Very well, my liege.

Hen. I have spoke long, be pleased yourself to say
How far you satisfied me.

Bis.   So please your highness,   210
The question did at first so stagger me,
Bearing a state of mighty moment in 't,
And consequence of dread, that I committed
The daring'st counsel which I had to doubt,
And did entreat your highness to this course

Which you are running here.

Hen.   I then mov'd you,
My Lord of Canterbury, and got your leave
To make this present summons : unsolicited
I left no reverend person in this court ;
But by particular consent proceeded   220
Under your hands and seals ; therefore, go on,
For no dislike i' the world against the person
Of the good queen ; but the sharp thorny points
Of my alleged reasons, drives this forward :
Prove but our marriage lawful, by my life
And kingly dignity, we are contented
To wear our mortal state to come with her
(Katharine our queen) before the primest creature
That 's paragon'd o' the world.

Cam.   So please your highness,
The queen being absent, 'tis a needful fitness   230
That we adjourn this court till further day ;
Meanwhile must be an earnest motion
Made to the queen to call back her appeal
She intends unto his holiness.

Hen.   (*aside*) I may perceive
These cardinals trifle with me : I abhor
This dilatory sloth, and tricks of Rome.
My learn'd and well-beloved servant, Cranmer,

Prithee return ; with thy approach, I know,
My comfort comes along.—Break up the court :
I say, set on.   240

Exeunt, in manner as they entered

Act Third

SCENE I

London.   The Queen's apartments

The Queen and her Women, as at work

Kat. Take thy lute, wench, my soul grows sad with troubles ;
Sing, and disperse 'em, if thou canst : leave working.

SONG

Orpheus with his lute made trees,
And the mountain tops that freeze,
  Bow themselves when he did sing :
To his music plants and flowers
Ever sprung, as sun and showers
  There had made a lasting spring.

Every thing that heard him play,
Even the billows of the sea,   10
  Hung their heads, and then lay by.

In sweet music is such art,
Killing care, and grief of heart,
Fall asleep, or hearing die.

Enter a Gentleman

Kat. How now?

Gent. An 't please your grace, the two great cardinals
Wait in the presence.

Kat.   Would they speak with me?

Gent. They will'd me say so, madam.

Kat.   Pray their graces
To come near.   (*exit Gent.*)   What can be their
    business
With me, a poor weak woman, fall'n from favour?   20
I do not like their coming: now I think on 't,
They should be good men, their affairs as righteous:
But all hoods make not monks.   †

Enter the two Cardinals, Wolsey and Campeius

Wol.   Peace to your highness!

Kat. Your graces find me here part of a housewife,
(I would be all) against the worst may happen:
What are your pleasures with me, reverend lords?

Wol. May it please you, noble madam, to withdraw
Into your private chamber; we shall give you
The full cause of our coming.

Kat.   Speak it here.
There's nothing I have done yet, o' my conscience,   30
Deserves a corner : would all other women
Could speak this with as free a soul as I do !
My lords, I care not (so much I am happy
Above a number) if my actions
Were tried by every tongue, every eye saw 'em,
Envy and base opinion set against 'em,
I know my life so even.   If your business
Seek me out, and that way I am wife in,
Out with it boldly : truth loves open dealing.

Wol. *Tanta est erga te mentis integritas, regina serenissima,—*   40
Kat. O good my lord, no Latin ;
I am not such a truant since my coming,
As not to know the language I have liv'd in :
A strange tongue makes my cause more strange,
        suspicious :
Pray speak in English ; here are some will thank you,
If you speak truth, for their poor mistress' sake ;
Believe me, she has had much wrong.   Lord cardinal,
The willing'st sin I ever yet committed
May be absolv'd in English.

Wol.   Noble lady,
I am sorry my integrity should breed,   50
(And service to his majesty and you)

70

So deep suspicion, where all faith was meant ;
We come not by the way of accusation,
To taint that honour every good tongue blesses ;
Nor to betray you any way to sorrow ;
You have too much, good lady : but to know
How you stand minded in the weighty difference
Between the king and you, and to deliver
(Like free and honest men) our just opinions,
And comforts to your cause.

Cam.   Most honour'd madam,   60
My Lord of York, out of his noble nature,
Zeal and obedience he still bore your grace,
Forgetting (like a good man) your late censure
Both of his truth and him (which was too far)
Offers, as I do, in a sign of peace,
His service, and his counsel.

Kat.   (*aside*) To betray me.—
My lords, I thank you both for your good wills,
Ye speak like honest men, (pray God ye prove so !)
But how to make ye suddenly an answer
In such a point of weight, so near mine honour,   70
(More near my life, I fear) with my weak wit,
And to such men of gravity and learning,
In truth I know not.   I was set at work,
Among my maids, full little, God knows, looking

71

Either for such men, or such business.
For her sake that I have been—for I feel
The last fit of my greatness—good your graces,
Let me have time and counsel for my cause :
Alas, I am a woman friendless, hopeless !

Wol. Madam, you wrong the king's love with these fears,   80
Your hopes and friends are infinite.

Kat.   In England
But little for my profit : can you think, lords,
That any Englishman dare give me counsel ?
Or be a known friend 'gainst his highness' pleasure,
(Though he be grown so desperate to be honest)
And live a subject ? Nay, forsooth, my friends,
They that must weigh out my afflictions,
They that my trust must grow to, live not here,
They are (as all my other comforts) far hence
In mine own country, lords.

Cam.   I would your grace   90
Would leave your griefs, and take my counsel.

Kat.   How, sir ?

Cam. Put your main cause into the king's protection,
He's loving and most gracious : 'twill be much
Both for your honour better, and your cause :
For if the trial of the law o'ertake ye,
You'll part away disgrac'd.

Wol.   He tells you rightly.

Kat. Ye tell me what ye wish for both, my ruin :
     Is this your Christian counsel ? out upon ye !
     Heaven is above all yet ; there sits a judge,
     That no king can corrupt.

Cam.   Your rage mistakes us.   100

Kat. The more shame for ye ; holy men I thought ye,
     Upon my soul, two reverend cardinal virtues ;
     But cardinal sins and hollow hearts I fear ye :
     Mend 'em, for shame, my lords.   Is this your comfort ?
     The cordial that ye bring a wretched lady ?
     A woman lost among ye, laugh'd at, scorn'd ?
     I will not wish ye half my miseries,
     I have more charity : but say, I warn'd ye ;
     Take heed, for heaven's sake take heed, lest at once
     The burthen of my sorrows fall upon ye.   110

Wol. Madam, this is a mere distraction ;
     You turn the good we offer into envy.

Kat. Ye turn me into nothing.   Woe upon ye,
     And all such false professors ! would you have me
     (If you have any justice, any pity,
     If ye be any thing but churchmen's habits)
     Put my sick cause into his hands that hates me ?
     Alas, has banish'd me his bed already,
     His love, too long ago !   I am old, my lords,

73

And all the fellowship I hold now with him 120
Is only my obedience.   What can happen
To me, above this wretchedness? all your studies
Make me a curse, like this.

Cam.   Your fears are worse.

Kat. Have I liv'd thus long (let me speak myself,
Since virtue finds no friends) a wife, a true one?
A woman (I dare say without vain-glory)
Never yet branded with suspicion?
Have I, with all my full affections,
Still met the king? lov'd him next heaven? obey'd
him?
Been (out of fondness) superstitious to him? 130
Almost forgot my prayers to content him?
And am I thus rewarded? 'tis not well, lords.
Bring me a constant woman to her husband,
One that ne'er dream'd a joy, beyond his pleasure;
And to that woman (when she has done most)
Yet will I add an honour; a great patience.

Wol. Madam, you wander from the good we aim at.

Kat. My lord, I dare not make myself so guilty,
To give up willingly that noble title
Your master wed me to: nothing but death 140
Shall e'er divorce my dignities.

Wol.   Pray, hear me.

74

Kat. Would I had never trod this English earth,
Or felt the flatteries that grow upon it !
Ye have angels' faces, but heaven knows your hearts.
What will become of me now, wretched lady ?
I am the most unhappy woman living.
Alas (poor wenches) where are now your fortunes ?
Shipwreck'd upon a kingdom, where no pity,
No friends, no hope, no kindred weep for me ?
Almost no grave allow'd me ?   Like the lily,   150
That once was mistress of the field, and flourish'd,
I 'll hang my head and perish.

Wol.   If your grace
Could but be brought to know our ends are honest,
You 'ld feel more comfort.   Why should we, good
     lady,
Upon what cause, wrong you ? alas, our places,
The way of our profession is against it :
We are to cure such sorrows, not to sow 'em.
For goodness' sake, consider what you do,
How you may hurt yourself ; ay, utterly
Grow from the king's acquaintance, by this carriage. 160
The hearts of princes kiss obedience,
So much they love it ; but to stubborn spirits,
They swell and grow, as terrible as storms.
I know you have a gentle, noble temper,

75

A soul as even as a calm ; pray think us
Those we profess, peace-makers, friends, and servants.
*Cam.*Madam, you 'll find it so ; you wrong your virtues
With these weak women's fears.   A noble spirit,
As yours was put into you, ever casts
Such doubts as false coin from it.   The king loves
    you,   170
Beware you lose it not : for us (if you please
To trust us in your business) we are ready
To use our utmost studies in your service.
Kat. Do what ye will, my lords : and pray forgive me ;
If I have us'd myself unmannerly,
You know I am a woman, lacking wit
To make a seemly answer to such persons.
Pray do my service to his majesty,
He has my heart yet, and shall have my prayers
While I shall have my life.   Come, reverend fathers, 180
Bestow your counsels on me.   She now begs
That little thought, when she set footing here,
She should have bought her dignities so dear.

                      Exeunt

SCENE II

Ante-chamber to the King's apartment

Enter the Duke of Norfolk, the Duke of Suffolk, the Earl of Surrey, and the Lord Chamberlain

Nor. If you will now unite in your complaints,
And force them with a constancy, the cardinal
Cannot stand under them.   If you omit
The offer of this time, I cannot promise
But that you shall sustain moe new disgraces,
With these you bear already.

Sur.   I am joyful
To meet the least occasion, that may give me
Remembrance of my father-in-law, the duke,
To be reveng'd on him.

Suf.   Which of the peers
Have uncontemn'd gone by him, or at least   10
Strangely neglected ?   when did he regard
The stamp of nobleness in any person
Out of himself ?

L.C.   My lords, you speak your pleasures :
What he deserves of you and me, I know ;
What we can do to him (though now the time
Gives way to us) I much fear.   If you cannot

77

Bar his access to the king, never attempt
Any thing on him ; for he hath a witchcraft
Over the king in 's tongue.

Nor.   O, fear him not,
His spell in that is out : the king hath found   20
Matter against him, that for ever mars
The honey of his language.   No, he 's settled
(Not to come off) in his displeasure.

Sur.   Sir,
I should be glad to hear such news as this
Once every hour.

Nor.   Believe it, this is true.
In the divorce, his contrary proceedings
Are all unfolded ; wherein he appears
As I would wish mine enemy.

Sur.   How came
His practices to light ?

Suf.   Most strangely.

Sur.   O, how, how ?

Suf. The cardinal's letters to the pope miscarried,   30
And came to the eye o' the king, wherein was read
How that the cardinal did entreat his holiness
To stay the judgement o' the divorce ; for if
It did take place, ' I do ' (quoth he) ' perceive
My king is tangled in affection, to

     A creature of the queen's, Lady Anne Bullen.'

Sur. Has the king this ?

Suf.   Believe it.

Sur.   Will this work ?

L.C. The king in this perceives him, how he coasts
    And hedges his own way.   But in this point
    All his tricks founder, and he brings his physic   40
    After his patient's death ; the king already
    Hath married the fair lady.

Sur.   Would he had !

Suf. May you be happy in your wish, my lord !
    For I profess you have it.

Sur.   Now, all my joy
    Trace the conjunction !

Suf.   My amen to 't !

Nor.   All men's !

Suf. There 's order given for her coronation :
    Marry, this is yet but young, and may be left
    To some ears unrecounted.   But, my lords,
    She is a gallant creature, and complete
    In mind and feature : I persuade me, from her   50
    Will fall some blessing to this land, which shall
    In it be memoriz'd.

Sur.   But will the king
    Digest this letter of the cardinal's ?

The Lord forbid !

Nor.　　　　　　　　Marry amen !

Suf.　　　　　　　　　　No, no :

There be moe wasps that buzz about his nose
Will make this sting the sooner.　Cardinal Campeius
Is stol'n away to Rome, hath ta'en no leave,
Has left the cause o' the king unhandled, and
Is posted as the agent of our cardinal,
To second all his plot.　I do assure you　　　　　60
The king cried ' Ha ! ' at this.

L.C.　　　　　　　　　　Now God incense him,
And let him cry ' Ha ! ' louder !

Nor.　　　　　　　　　　But, my lord,
When returns Cranmer ?

Suf. He is return'd in his opinions, which　　　　†
Have satisfied the king for his divorce,
Together with all famous colleges
Almost in Christendom : shortly, I believe,
His second marriage shall be publish'd, and
Her coronation.　Katharine no more
Shall be call'd queen, but princess dowager　　　70
And widow to Prince Arthur.

Nor.　　　　　　　　　　This same Cranmer 's
A worthy fellow, and hath ta'en much pain
In the king's business.

Suf.   He has, and we shall see him
    For it an archbishop.

Nor.   So I hear.

Suf.   'Tis so.
    The cardinal !

          Enter Wolsey and Cromwell

Nor.   Observe, observe, he 's moody.

Wol. The packet, Cromwell,
    Gave 't you the king ?

Cro.   To his own hand, in 's bedchamber.

Wol. Look'd he o' the inside of the paper ?

Cro.   Presently
    He did unseal them, and the first he view'd,
    He did it with a serious mind ; a heed   80
    Was in his countenance.   You he bade
    Attend him here this morning.

Wol.   Is he ready
    To come abroad ?

Cro.   I think by this he is.

Wol. Leave me awhile.   *Exit Cromwell*
    (*aside*) It shall be to the Duchess of Alençon,
    The French king's sister ; he shall marry her.
    Anne Bullen ?   No ; I 'll no Anne Bullens for him,
    There 's more in 't than fair visage.   Bullen ?
    No, we 'll no Bullens.   Speedily I wish ·

To hear from Rome.   The Marchioness of Pembroke?
Nor. He's discontented.
Suf.   May be he hears the king   91
Does whet his anger to him.
Sur.   Sharp enough,
Lord, for thy justice!
Wol. (*aside*) The late queen's gentlewoman?   A knight's
          daughter
To be her mistress' mistress? the queen's queen?
This candle burns not clear, 'tis I must snuff it,
Then out it goes.   What though I know her virtuous
And well deserving? yet I know her for
A spleeny Lutheran, and not wholesome to
Our cause, that she should lie i' the bosom of   100
Our hard-rul'd king.   Again, there is sprung up
An heretic, an arch one; Cranmer, one
Hath crawl'd into the favour of the king,
And is his oracle.
Nor.   He is vex'd at something.
Sur. I would 'twere something that would fret the string,
The master-cord on 's heart!
          Enter King, reading of a schedule, and Lovell
Suf.   The king, the king!
Hen. What piles of wealth hath he accumulated
To his own portion! and what expense by the hour

Seems to flow from him !   How, i' the name of thrift,
Does he rake this together ?   Now, my lords,   110
Saw you the cardinal ?

Nor.   My lord, we have
Stood here observing him.   Some strange commotion
Is in his brain : he.bites his lip, and starts,
Stops on a sudden, looks upon the ground,
Then lays his finger on his temple ; straight
Springs out into fast gait, then stops again,
Strikes his breast hard, and anon, he casts
His eye against the moon : in most strange postures
We have seen him set himself.

Hen.   It may well be,
There is a mutiny in 's mind.   This morning   120
Papers of state he sent me, to peruse
As I requir'd : and wot you what I found
(There on my conscience, put unwittingly) ?
Forsooth, an inventory, thus importing,
The several parcels of his plate, his treasure,
Rich stuffs and ornaments of household, which
I find at such proud rate, that it out-speaks
Possession of a subject.

Nor.   It 's heaven's will,
Some spirit put this paper in the packet,
To bless your eye withal.

Hen.   If we did think   130
        His contemplation were above the earth,
        And fix'd on spiritual object, he should still
        Dwell in his musings, but I am afraid
        His thinkings are below the moon, not worth
        His serious considering.

                          King takes his seat ; whispers Lovell,
                                who goes to the Cardinal

Wol.   Heaven forgive me !
        Ever God bless your highness !

Hen.   Good my lord,
        You are full of heavenly stuff, and bear the inventory
        Of your best graces in your mind ; the which
        You were now running o'er : you have scarce time
        To steal from spiritual leisure a brief span   140
        To keep your earthly audit, sure, in that
        I deem you an ill husband, and am glad
        To have you therein my companion.

Wol.   Sir,
        For holy offices I have a time ; a time
        To think upon the part of business, which
        I bear i' the state ; and nature does require
        Her times of preservation, which perforce
        I, her frail son, amongst my brethren mortal,
        Must give my tendance to.

                              84

Hen.   You have said well.

Wol. And ever may your highness yoke together,   150
    (As I will lend you cause) my doing well
    With my well saying !

Hen.   'Tis well said again,
    And 'tis a kind of good deed to say well,
    And yet words are no deeds.   My father lov'd you,
    He said he did, and with his deed did crown
    His word upon you.   Since I had my office,
    I have kept you next my heart, have not alone
    Employ'd you where high profits might come home,
    But par'd my present havings, to bestow
    My bounties upon you.

Wol.   (*aside*) What should this mean ?   160

Sur. (*aside*) The Lord increase this business !

Hen.   Have I not made you
    The prime man of the state ?   I pray you tell me,
    If what I now pronounce you have found true :
    And, if you may confess it, say withal,
    If you are bound to us, or no.   What say you ?

Wol. My sovereign, I confess your royal graces,
    Shower'd on me daily, have been more than could
    My studied purposes requite, which went
    Beyond all man's endeavours.   My endeavours
    Have ever come too short of my desires,   170

Yet fil'd with my abilities : mine own ends
Have been mine so, that evermore they pointed
To the good of your most sacred person, and
The profit of the state.　For your great graces
Heap'd upon me (poor undeserver) I
Can nothing render but allegiant thanks,
My prayers to heaven for you, my loyalty,
Which ever has, and ever shall be growing,
Till death (that winter) kill it.

Hen.　　　　　　　　　　　Fairly answer'd ;
A loyal and obedient subject is　　　　　　　　　180
Therein illustrated, the honour of it
Does pay the act of it, as, i' the contrary,
The foulness is the punishment.　I presume
That, as my hand has open'd bounty to you,
My heart dropp'd love, my power rain'd honour, more
On you than any ; so your hand, and heart,
Your brain, and every function of your power,
Should, notwithstanding that your bond of duty,
As 'twere in love's particular, be more
To me, your friend, than any.

Wol.　　　　　　　　I do profess　　　　　190
That for your highness' good I ever labour'd
More than mine own ; that am, have, and will be　　†
(Though all the world should crack their duty to you,

And throw it from their soul, though perils did
Abound, as thick as thought could make 'em, and
Appear in forms more horrid) yet my duty,
As doth a rock against the chiding flood,
Should the approach of this wild river break,
And stand unshaken yours.

Hen.   'Tis nobly spoken :
Take notice, lords, he has a loyal breast,   200
For you have seen him open 't.   (*Giving him papers.*)
    Read o'er this,
And after, this, and then to breakfast with
What appetite you have.

> *Exit King, frowning upon the Cardinal : the nobles*
>   *throng after him, smiling and whispering*

Wol.   What should this mean ?
What sudden anger 's this ? how have I reap'd it ?
He parted frowning from me, as if ruin
Leap'd from his eyes.   So looks the chafed lion
Upon the daring huntsman that has gall'd him ;
Then makes him nothing.   I must read this paper ;
I fear, the story of his anger.   'Tis so ;
This paper has undone me : 'tis the account   210
Of all that world of wealth I have drawn together
For mine own ends, (indeed, to gain the popedom,
And fee my friends in Rome.)   O negligence !

Fit for a fool to fall by : what cross devil
Made me put this main secret in the packet
I sent the king ?   Is there no way to cure this ?
No new device to beat this from his brains ?
I know 'twill stir him strongly ; yet I know
A way, if it take right, in spite of fortune
Will bring me off again.   What 's this ?   ' To the
    Pope ? '   220
The letter, as I live, with all the business
I writ to 's holiness.   Nay then, farewell !
I have touch'd the highest point of all my greatness,
And from that full meridian of my glory,
I haste now to my setting.   I shall fall
Like a bright exhalation in the evening,
And no man see me more.

Re-enter to Wolsey the Dukes of Norfolk and Suffolk, the
    Earl of Surrey, and the Lord Chamberlain

Nor. Hear the king's pleasure, cardinal, who commands you
    To render up the great seal presently
    Into our hands, and to confine yourself   230
    To Asher-house, my Lord of Winchester's,
    Till you hear further from his highness.

Wol.   Stay :
    Where 's your commission, lords ? words cannot carry
    Authority so weighty.

Suf.   Who dare cross 'em,
    Bearing the king's will from his mouth expressly?

Wol. Till I find more than will or words to do it
    (I mean your malice) know, officious lords,
    I dare, and must deny it.   Now I feel
    Of what coarse metal ye are moulded, envy,
    How eagerly ye follow my disgraces,   240
    As if it fed ye, and how sleek and wanton
    Ye appear in every thing may bring my ruin!
    Follow your envious courses, men of malice;
    You have Christian warrant for 'em, and no doubt
    In time will find their fit rewards.   That seal
    You ask with such a violence, the king
    (Mine and your master) with his own hand gave me;
    Bade me enjoy it, with the place and honours,
    During my life; and, to confirm his goodness,
    Tied it by letters-patents.   Now, who'll take it?   250

Sur. The king that gave it.

Wol.   It must be himself then.

Sur. Thou art a proud traitor, priest.

Wol.   Proud lord, thou liest:
    Within these forty hours Surrey durst better
    Have burnt that tongue than said so.

Sur.   Thy ambition
    (Thou scarlet sin) robb'd this bewailing land

Of noble Buckingham, my father-in-law ;
The heads of all thy brother cardinals,
(With thee, and all thy best parts bound together)
Weigh'd not a hair of his.   Plague of your policy !
You sent me deputy for Ireland,   260
Far from his succour, from the king, from all
That might have mercy on the fault thou gav'st him ;
Whilst your great goodness, out of holy pity,
Absolv'd him with an axe.

Wol.   This, and all else
This talking lord can lay upon my credit,
I answer, is most false.   The duke by law
Found his deserts.   How innocent I was
From any private malice in his end,
His noble jury and foul cause can witness.
If I lov'd many words, lord, I should tell you   270
You have as little honesty as honour,
That in the way of loyalty and truth
Toward the king, my ever royal master,
Dare mate a sounder man than Surrey can be,
And all that love his follies.

Sur.   By my soul,
Your long coat, priest, protects you, thou shouldst feel
My sword i' the life-blood of thee else.   My lords,
Can ye endure to hear this arrogance ?

And from this fellow ?   If we live thus tamely,
To be thus jaded by a piece of scarlet,   †
Farewell nobility ; let his grace go forward,   281
And dare us with his cap, like larks.

Wol.   All goodness
Is poison to thy stomach.

Sur.   Yes, that goodness
Of gleaning all the land's wealth into one,
Into your own hands, cardinal, by extortion ;
The goodness of your intercepted packets
You writ to the pope, against the king : your goodness,
Since you provoke me, shall be most notorious.
My Lord of Norfolk, as you are truly noble,
As you respect the common good, the state   290
Of our despis'd nobility, our issues,
(Who, if he live, will scarce be gentlemen)
Produce the grand sum of his sins, the articles
Collected from his life.   I'll startle you
Worse than the sacring bell, when the brown wench
Lay kissing in your arms, lord cardinal.

Wol. How much, methinks, I could despise this man,
But that I am bound in charity against it !

Nor. Those articles, my lord, are in the king's hand:
But, thus much, they are foul ones.

Wol.   So much fairer   300

And spotless shall mine innocence arise,
When the king knows my truth.

Sur.   This cannot save you :
I thank my memory, I yet remember
Some of these articles, and out they shall.
Now, if you can blush, and cry ' guilty,' cardinal,
You 'll show a little honesty.

Wol.   Speak on, sir,
I dare your worst objections : if I blush,
It is to see a nobleman want manners.

Sur. I had rather want those than my head ; have at you !
First, that without the king's assent or knowledge,   310
You wrought to be a legate, by which power
You maim'd the jurisdiction of all bishops.

Nor. Then, that in all your writ to Rome, or else
To foreign princes, *Ego et Rex meus*
Was still inscrib'd ; in which you brought the king
To be your servant.

Suf.   Then, that without the knowledge
Either of king or council, when you went
Ambassador to the emperor, you made bold
To carry into Flanders the great seal.

Sur. Item, you sent a large commission   320
To Gregory de Cassado, to conclude,
Without the king's will, or the state's allowance,

A league between his highness and Ferrara.

Suf. That out of mere ambition, you have caus'd
    Your holy hat to be stamp'd on the king's coin.

Sur. Then, that you have sent innumerable substance,
    (By what means got, I leave to your own conscience)
    To furnish Rome, and to prepare the ways
    You have for dignities, to the mere undoing
    Of all the kingdom.   Many more there are,   330
    Which since they are of you, and odious,
    I will not taint my mouth with.

L.C.   O my lord,
    Press not a falling man too far ; 'tis virtue :
    His faults lie open to the laws, let them,
    (Not you) correct him.   My heart weeps to see him
    So little of his great self.

Sur.   I forgive him.

Suf. Lord cardinal, the king's further pleasure is,
    Because all those things you have done of late
    By your power legative within this kingdom,
    Fall into the compass of a præmunire,   340
    That therefore such a writ be sued against you,
    To forfeit all your goods, lands, tenements,
    Chattels, and whatsoever, and to be
    Out of the king's protection.   This is my charge.

Nor. And so we 'll leave you to your meditations

How to live better.   For your stubborn answer
About the giving back the great seal to us,
The king shall know it, and (no doubt) shall thank
     you.
So fare you well, my little good lord cardinal.

Exeunt all but Wolsey

Wol. So farewell, to the little good you bear me.   350
Farewell? a long farewell to all my greatness!
This is the state of man: to-day he puts forth
The tender leaves of hopes, to-morrow blossoms,
And bears his blushing honours thick upon him;
The third day, comes a frost, a killing frost,
And when he thinks, good easy man, full surely
His greatness is a-ripening, nips his root,
And then he falls as I do.   I have ventur'd
Like little wanton boys that swim on bladders,
This many summers in a sea of glory,   360
But far beyond my depth: my high-blown pride
At length broke under me, and now has left me
Weary, and old with service, to the mercy
Of a rude stream, that must for ever hide me.
Vain pomp, and glory of this world, I hate ye:
I feel my heart new open'd.   O, how wretched
Is that poor man that hangs on princes' favours!
There is betwixt that smile we would aspire to,

That sweet aspect of princes, and their ruin,

More pangs and fears than wars or women have :   370

And when he falls, he falls like Lucifer,

Never to hope again.

Enter Cromwell, and stands amazed

                Why, how now, Cromwell ?

Cro. I have no power to speak, sir.

Wol.   What, amaz'd

At my misfortunes ? can thy spirit wonder

A great man should decline ?   Nay, an you weep,

I am fall'n indeed.

Cro.   How does your grace ?

Wol.   Why, well ;

Never so truly happy, my good Cromwell ;

I know myself now, and I feel within me

A peace above all earthly dignities,

A still and quiet conscience.   The king has cur'd me,   380

I humbly thank his grace ; and from these shoulders,

These ruin'd pillars, out of pity, taken

A load would sink a navy—too much honour.

O, 'tis a burden, Cromwell, 'tis a burden

Too heavy for a man that hopes for heaven !

Cro. I am glad your grace has made that right use of it.

Wol. I hope I have : I am able now, methinks,

Out of a fortitude of soul I feel,

To endure more miseries, and greater far,
Than my weak-hearted enemies dare offer.   390
What news abroad ?

Cro.   The heaviest, and the worst,
Is your displeasure with the king.

Wol.   God bless him !

Cro. The next is, that Sir Thomas More is chosen
Lord chancellor in your place.

Wol.   That 's somewhat sudden :
But he 's a learned man.   May he continue
Long in his highness' favour, and do justice
For truth's sake, and his conscience ; that his bones,
When he has run his course, and sleeps in blessings,
May have a tomb of orphans' tears wept on him !
What more ?

Cro.   That Cranmer is return'd with welcome ;   400
Install'd lord archbishop of Canterbury.

Wol. That 's news indeed.

Cro.   Last, that the Lady Anne,
Whom the king hath in secrecy long married,
This day was view'd in open, as his queen,
Going to chapel ; and the voice is now
Only about her coronation.

Wol. There was the weight that pull'd me down.   O
     Cromwell,

The king has gone beyond me : all my glories
In that one woman I have lost for ever.
No sun shall ever usher forth mine honours,   410
Or gild again the noble troops that waited
Upon my smiles.   Go, get thee from me, Cromwell,
I am a poor fall'n man, unworthy now
To be thy lord and master.   Seek the king ;
(That sun, I pray, may never set) I have told him
What, and how true thou art ; he will advance thee :
Some little memory of me will stir him
(I know his noble nature) not to let
Thy hopeful service perish too.   Good Cromwell,
Neglect him not ; make use now, and provide   420
For thine own future safety.

Cro.   O my lord,
Must I then leave you ? must I needs forgo
So good, so noble, and so true a master ?
Bear witness, all that have not hearts of iron,
With what a sorrow Cromwell leaves his lord.
The king shall have my service ; but my prayers
For ever and for ever shall be yours.

Wol. Cromwell, I did not think to shed a tear
In all my miseries ; but thou hast forc'd me,
(Out of thy honest truth) to play the woman.   430
Let's dry our eyes : and thus far hear me, Cromwell,

And when I am forgotten, as I shall be,
And sleep in dull cold marble, where no mention
Of me more must be heard of, say I taught thee ;
Say Wolsey, that once trod the ways of glory,
And sounded all the depths and shoals of honour,
Found thee a way (out of his wreck) to rise in ;
A sure and safe one, though thy master miss'd it.
Mark but my fall, and that that ruin'd me :
Cromwell, I charge thee, fling away ambition,   440
By that sin fell the angels ; how can man then
(The image of his Maker) hope to win by it ?
Love thyself last, cherish those hearts that hate thee ;
Corruption wins not more than honesty.
Still in thy right hand carry gentle peace
To silence envious tongues.   Be just, and fear not ;
Let all the ends thou aim'st at be thy country's,
Thy God's, and truth's.   Then if thou fall'st, O Cromwell,
Thou fall'st a blessed martyr !   Serve the king ;
And prithee lead me in :   450
There take an inventory of all I have,
To the last penny, 'tis the king's.   My robe,
And my integrity to heaven, is all
I dare now call mine own.   Cromwell, Cromwell !
Had I but serv'd my God with half the zeal

I sery'd my king, he would not in mine age
Have left me naked to mine enemies.
Cro. Good sir, have patience.
Wol.   So I have.   Farewell
The hopes of court ; my hopes in heaven do dwell.

                                Exeunt

Act Fourth

SCENE I

A street in Westminster

Enter two Gentlemen, meeting one another

1.*G.* You're well met once again.
2.*G.*   So are you.
1.*G.* You come to take your stand here, and behold
The Lady Anne pass from her coronation ?
2.*G.* 'Tis all my business.   At our last encounter,
The Duke of Buckingham came from his trial.
1.*G.* 'Tis very true : but that time offer'd sorrow,
This, general joy.
2.*G.*   'Tis well : the citizens
I am sure have shown at full their royal minds—

As, let 'em have their rights, they are ever forward—
In celebration of this day with shows,   10
Pageants, and sights of honour.   †

1.G.   Never greater,
Nor, I'll assure you, better taken, sir.

2.G. May I be bold to ask what that contains,
That paper in your hand?

1.G.   Yes, 'tis the list
Of those that claim their offices this day,
By custom of the coronation.
The Duke of Suffolk is the first, and claims
To be high-steward; next the Duke of Norfolk,
He to be earl marshal: you may read the rest.

2.G. I thank you, sir: had I not known those customs,   20
I should have been beholding to your paper.
But, I beseech you, what's become of Katharine,
The princess dowager? how goes her business?

1.G. That I can tell you too.   The Archbishop
Of Canterbury, accompanied with other
Learned and reverend fathers of his order,
Held a late court at Dunstable, six miles off
From Ampthill, where the princess lay, to which
She was often cited by them, but appear'd not:
And, to be short, for not appearance, and   30
The king's late scruple, by the main assent

Of all these learned men she was divorc'd,
And the late marriage made of none effect:
Since which, she was remov'd to Kimbolton,
Where she remains now sick.

2.G.   Alas, good lady!

Trumpets

The trumpets sound: stand close, the queen is coming.

Hautboys

THE ORDER OF THE CORONATION

1. *A lively Flourish of Trumpets.*
2. *Then, two Judges.*
3. *Lord Chancellor, with purse and mace before him.*
4. *Choristers, singing.*   *Music.*
5. *Mayor of London, bearing the mace. Then Garter, in his coat of arms, and on his head he wears a gilt copper crown.*
6. *Marquess Dorset, bearing a sceptre of gold, on his head a demi-coronal of gold. With him, the Earl of Surrey, bearing the rod of silver with the dove, crowned with an earl's coronet. Collars of Esses.*
7. *Duke of Suffolk, in his robe of estate, his coronet on his head, bearing a long white wand, as high-steward. With him, the Duke of Norfolk, with the rod of marshalship, a coronet on his head. Collars of Esses.*
8. *A canopy borne by four of the Cinque-ports; under it, the*

15 h

> *Queen in her robe, in her hair, richly adorned with pearl,*
> *crowned. On each side her, the Bishops of London and*
> *Winchester.*

9. *The old Duchess of Norfolk, in a coronal of gold, wrought*
   with flowers, bearing the Queen's train.

10. *Certain Ladies or Countesses, with plain circlets of gold*
    without flowers.
    They pass over the stage in order and state.

2.*G.* A royal train, believe me. These I know:
Who's that that bears the sceptre?

1.*G.*   Marquess Dorset:
And that the Earl of Surrey, with the rod.

2.*G.* A bold brave gentleman. That should be   40
The Duke of Suffolk.

1.*G.*   'Tis the same: high-steward.

2.*G.* And that my Lord of Norfolk?

1.*G.*   Yes.

2.*G.*   (*looking on the Queen*) Heaven bless thee!
Thou hast the sweetest face I ever look'd on.
Sir, as I have a soul, she is an angel;
Our king has all the Indies in his arms,
And more, and richer, when he strains that lady;
I cannot blame his conscience.

1.*G.*   They that bear
The cloth of honour over her, are four barons

Of the Cinque-ports.

2.*G.* Those men are happy, and so are all are near her.   50
   I take it, she that carries up the train
   Is that old noble lady, Duchess of Norfolk.

1.*G.* It is, and all the rest are countesses.

2.*G.* Their coronets say so.   These are stars indeed,
   And sometimes falling ones.

1.*G.*   No more of that.

Exit procession ; and then a great flourish of trumpets
Enter a third Gentleman

   God save you, sir ! where have you been broiling ?

3.*G.* Among the crowd i' the abbey, where a finger
   Could not be wedg'd in more : I am stifled
   With the mere rankness of their joy.

2.*G.*   You saw
   The ceremony ?   60

3.*G.* That I did.

1.*G.*   How was it ?

3.*G.* Well worth the seeing.

2.*G.*   Good sir, speak it to us.

3.*G.* As well as I am able.   The rich stream
   Of lords and ladies, having brought the queen
   To a prepar'd place in the choir, fell off
   A distance from her ; while her grace sat down
   To rest awhile, some half an hour or so,

In a rich chair of state, opposing freely
The beauty of her person to the people.
Believe me, sir, she is the goodliest woman   70
That ever lay by man : which when the people
Had the full view of, such a noise arose
As the shrouds make at sea, in a stiff tempest,
As loud, and to as many tunes : hats, cloaks,
(Doublets, I think) flew up, and had their faces
Been loose, this day they had been lost.   Such joy
I never saw before.   Great-bellied women,
That had not half a week to go, like rams
In the old time of war, would shake the press,
And make 'em reel before 'em.   No man living   80
Could say ' This is my wife ' there, all were woven
So strangely in one piece.

2.*G.*   But what follow'd ?

3.*G.* At length, her grace rose, and with modest paces
Came to the altar, where she kneel'd, and saintlike
Cast her fair eyes to heaven, and pray'd devoutly.
Then rose again, and bow'd her to the people ;
When by the Archbishop of Canterbury
She had all the royal makings of a queen ;
As holy oil, Edward Confessor's crown,
The rod, and bird of peace, and all such emblems   90
Laid nobly on her : which perform'd, the choir,

With all the choicest music of the kingdom,
Together sung ' Te Deum.'   So she parted,
And with the same full state pac'd back again
To York-place, where the feast is held.

1.*G.*   Sir,
You must no more call it York-place, that's past ;
For since the cardinal fell, that title's lost,
'Tis now the king's, and call'd Whitehall.

3.*G.*   I know it ;
But 'tis so lately alter'd, that the old name
Is fresh about me.

2.*G.*   What two reverend bishops   100
Were those that went on each side of the queen ?

3.*G.* Stokesly and Gardiner, the one of Winchester,
Newly preferr'd from the king's secretary ;
The other London.

2.*G.*   He of Winchester
Is held no great good lover of the archbishop's,
The virtuous Cranmer.

3.*G.*   All the land knows that :
However, yet there is no great breach, when it comes,
Cranmer will find a friend will not shrink from him.

2.*G.* Who may that be, I pray you ?

3.*G.*   Thomas Cromwell,
A man in much esteem with the king, and truly   110

A worthy friend.   The king has made him master
O' the jewel house,
And one already of the privy council.

2.G. He will deserve more.

3.G.   Yes, without all doubt.
Come, gentlemen, ye shall go my way,
Which is to the court, and there ye shall be my guests :
Something I can command.   As I walk thither,
I'll tell ye more.

Both.   You may command us, sir.   *Exeunt*

SCENE II

Kimbolton

*Enter Katharine Dowager, sick, led between Griffith, her
Gentleman Usher, and Patience, her woman*

Gri. How does your grace ?

Kat.   O Griffith, sick to death !
My legs like loaden branches bow to the earth,
Willing to leave their burthen ; reach a chair :
So now, methinks, I feel a little ease.
Didst thou not tell me, Griffith, as thou led'st me,
That the great child of honour, Cardinal Wolsey,
Was dead ?

Gri.   Yes, madam ; but I think your grace,
       Out of the pain you suffer'd, gave no ear to 't.

Kat. Prithee, good Griffith, tell me how he died :
       If well, he stepp'd before me happily   10
       For my example.

Gri.   Well, the voice goes, madam,
       For after the stout Earl Northumberland
       Arrested him at York, and brought him forward,
       As a man sorely tainted, to his answer,
       He fell sick suddenly, and grew so ill
       He could not sit his mule.

Kat.   Alas, poor man !

Gri. At last, with easy roads, he came to Leicester,
       Lodg'd in the abbey ; where the reverend abbot,
       With all his covent, honourably receiv'd him ;
       To whom he gave these words, ' O father abbot,   20
       An old man, broken with the storms of state,
       Is come to lay his weary bones among ye ;
       Give him a little earth for charity ! '
       So went to bed ; where eagerly his sickness
       Pursued him still, and three nights after this,
       About the hour of eight, which he himself
       Foretold should be his last, full of repentance,
       Continual meditations, tears, and sorrows,
       He gave his honours to the world again,

His blessed part to heaven, and slept in peace.   30

Kat. So may he rest, his faults lie gently on him!
    Yet thus far, Griffith, give me leave to speak him,
    And yet with charity.   He was a man
    Of an unbounded stomach, ever ranking
    Himself with princes.   One that by suggestion
    Tied all the kingdom.   Simony was fair-play,
    His own opinion was his law.   I' the presence
    He would say untruths, and be ever double
    Both in his words, and meaning.   He was never
    (But where he meant to ruin) pitiful.   40
    His promises were, as he then was, mighty:
    But his performance, as he is now, nothing:
    Of his own body he was ill, and gave
    The clergy ill example.

Gri.   Noble madam,
    Men's evil manners live in brass, their virtues
    We write in water.   May it please your highness
    To hear me speak his good now?

Kat.   Yes, good Griffith,
    I were malicious else.

Gri.   This cardinal,
    Though from an humble stock, undoubtedly
    Was fashion'd to much honour.   From his cradle   50
    He was a scholar, and a ripe and good one:

Exceeding wise, fair-spoken, and persuading :
Lofty, and sour to them that lov'd him not :
But, to those men that sought him, sweet as summer.
And though he were unsatisfied in getting
(Which was a sin) yet in bestowing, madam,
He was most princely : ever witness for him
Those twins of learning, that he rais'd in you,
Ipswich and Oxford ! one of which, fell with him,
Unwilling to outlive the good that did it ;   60
The other (though unfinish'd) yet so famous,
So excellent in art ; and still so rising,
That Christendom shall ever speak his virtue.
His overthrow heap'd happiness upon him :
For then, and not till then, he felt himself,
And found the blessedness of being little.
And, to add greater honours to his age
Than man could give him, he died, fearing God.

Kat. After my death, I wish no other herald,
No other speaker of my living actions,   70
To keep mine honour from corruption,
But such an honest chronicler as Griffith.
Whom I most hated living, thou hast made me,
With thy religious truth, and modesty,
(Now in his ashes) honour : peace be with him !
Patience, be near me still, and set me lower.

I have not long to trouble thee.   Good Griffith,
Cause the musicians play me that sad note
I nam'd my knell; whilst I sit meditating
On that celestial harmony I go to.   80

Sad and solemn music

Gri. She is asleep : good wench, let's sit down quiet,
For fear we wake her.   Softly, gentle Patience.

The Vision

*Enter solemnly tripping one after another, six person-
ages, clad in white robes, wearing on their heads garlands
of bays, and golden vizards on their faces, branches of bays
or palm in their hands.   They first congee unto her, then
dance : and, at certain changes, the first two hold a spare
garland over her head, at which the other four make
reverent curtsies.   Then the two that held the garland
deliver the same to the other next two, who observe the
same order in their changes, and holding the garland over
her head.   Which done, they deliver the same garland to
the last two, who likewise observe the same order.   At
which (as it were by inspiration) she makes (in her sleep)
signs of rejoicing, and holdeth up her hands to heaven.
And so in their dancing vanish, carrying the garland with
them.   The music continues.*

Kat. Spirits of peace, where are ye ? are ye all gone ?

And leave me here in wretchedness, behind ye?

Gri. Madam, we are here.

Kat.　　　　　　It is not you I call for,
Saw ye none enter since I slept?

Gri.　　　　　　　　None, madam.

Kat. No?   Saw you not even now a blessed troop
Invite me to a banquet, whose bright faces
Cast thousand beams upon me, like the sun?
They promis'd me eternal happiness,　　　　　90
And brought me garlands, Griffith, which I feel
I am not worthy yet to wear: I shall, assuredly.

Gri. I am most joyful, madam, such good dreams
Possess your fancy.

Kat.　　　　　　Bid the music leave,
They are harsh and heavy to me.　　　*Music ceases*

Pat.　　　　　　　Do you note
How much her grace is alter'd on the sudden?
How long her face is drawn? how pale she looks
And of an earthy cold?   Mark her eyes!

Gri. She is going, wench.   Pray, pray.

Pat.　　　　　　Heaven comfort her

Enter a Messenger

Mes. An't like your grace,—

Kat.　　　　　　You are a saucy fellow,　　　100
Deserve we no more reverence?

Gri.   You are to blame.
     Knowing she will not lose her wonted greatness,
     To use so rude behaviour : go to, kneel.

Mes. I humbly do entreat your highness' pardon,
     My haste made me unmannerly.   There is staying
     A gentleman, sent from the king, to see you.

Kat. Admit him entrance, Griffith.   But this fellow
     Let me ne'er see again.

                     Exeunt Griffith and Messenger
                Re-enter Griffith, with Capucius
                         If my sight fail not,
     You should be lord ambassador from the emperor,
     My royal nephew, and your name Capucius.   110

Cap. Madam, the same ; your servant.

Kat.   O, my lord,
     The times and titles now are alter'd strangely
     With me, since first you knew me.   But, I pray you,
     What is your pleasure with me ?

Cap.   Noble lady,
     First, mine own service to your grace, the next,
     The king's request, that I would visit you,
     Who grieves much for your weakness, and by me
     Sends you his princely commendations,
     And heartily entreats you take good comfort.

Kat. O my good lord, that comfort comes too late,   120

'Tis like a pardon after execution;
That gentle physic, given in time, had cur'd me:
But now I am past all comforts here, but prayers.
How does his highness?

Cap.   Madam, in good health.

Kat. So may he ever do, and ever flourish,
When I shall dwell with worms, and my poor name
Banish'd the kingdom!   Patience, is that letter
I caus'd you write, yet sent away?

Pat.   No, madam.

                    Giving it to Katharine

Kat. Sir, I most humbly pray you to deliver
This to my lord the king.

Cap.   Most willing, madam.   130

Kat. In which I have commended to his goodness
The model of our chaste loves, his young daughter—
The dews of heaven fall thick in blessings on her!—
Beseeching him to give her virtuous breeding.
She is young, and of a noble modest nature,
I hope she will deserve well; and a little
To love her for her mother's sake, that lov'd him,
Heaven knows how dearly.   My next poor petition
Is that his noble grace would have some pity
Upon my wretched women, that so long   140
Have follow'd both my fortunes, faithfully,

Of which there is not one, I dare avow,
(And now I should not lie) but will deserve,
For virtue, and true beauty of the soul,
For honesty, and decent carriage,
A right good husband (let him be a noble)
And sure those men are happy that shall have 'em.
The last is for my men, they are the poorest,
(But poverty could never draw 'em from me)
That they may have their wages, duly paid 'em,   150
And something over to remember me by.
If heaven had pleas'd to have given me longer life
And able means, we had not parted thus.
These are the whole contents, and, good my lord,
By that you love the dearest in this world,
As you wish Christian peace to souls departed,
Stand these poor people's friend, and urge the king
To do me this last right.

Cap.   By heaven I will,
Or let me lose the fashion of a man !

Kat. I thank you, honest lord.   Remember me   160
In all humility unto his highness :
Say his long trouble now is passing
Out of this world.   Tell him in death I bless'd him,
For so I will.   Mine eyes grow dim.   Farewell,
My lord.   Griffith, farewell.   Nay, Patience,

You must not leave me yet.   I must to bed,
Call in more women.   When I am dead, good wench,
Let me be us'd with honour ; strew me over
With maiden flowers, that all the world may know
I was a chaste wife, to my grave : embalm me,   170
Then lay me forth (although unqueen'd) yet like
A queen, and daughter to a king, inter me.
I can no more.   *Exeunt, leading Katharine*

Act Fifth

SCENE I

London.   A gallery in the palace

*Enter Gardiner, Bishop of Winchester, a Page with a torch
before him, met by Sir Thomas Lovell*

Gar. It 's one o'clock, boy, is 't not ?
Boy.   It hath struck.
Gar. These should be hours for necessities,
Not for delights ; times to repair our nature
With comforting repose, and not for us
To waste these times.   Good hour of night, Sir
Thomas !

Whither so late ?

Lov.   Came you from the king, my lord ?

Gar. I did, Sir Thomas, and left him at primero
    With the Duke of Suffolk.

Lov.   I must to him too,
    Before he go to bed. I 'll take my leave.

Gar. Not yet, Sir Thomas Lovell. What 's the matter ?   10
    It seems you are in haste : an if there be
    No great offence belongs to 't, give your friend
    Some touch of your late business : affairs that walk
    (As they say spirits do) at midnight, have
    In them a wilder nature than the business
    That seeks dispatch by day.

Lov.   My lord, I love you ;
    And durst commend a secret to your ear
    Much weightier than this work. The queen 's in
        labour,
    They say in great extremity, and fear'd
    She 'll with the labour end.

Gar.   The fruit she goes with   20
    I pray for heartily, that it may find
    Good time, and live : but for the stock, Sir Thomas,
    I wish it grubb'd up now.

Lov.   Methinks I could
    Cry the amen, and yet my conscience says

She's a good creature, and, sweet lady, does
Deserve our better wishes.

Gar.   But, sir, sir,
Hear me, Sir Thomas, you're a gentleman
Of mine own way ; I know you wise, religious ;
And, let me tell you, it will ne'er be well,
'Twill not, Sir Thomas Lovell, take 't of me,   30
Till Cranmer, Cromwell, her two hands, and she,
Sleep in their graves.

Lov.   Now, sir, you speak of two
The most remark'd i' the kingdom : as for Cromwell,
Beside that of the jewel house, is made master
O' the rolls, and the king's secretary ; further, sir,
Stands in the gap and trade of moe preferments,
With which the time will load him.   The archbishop
Is the king's hand, and tongue, and who dare speak
One syllable against him ?

Gar.   Yes, yes, Sir Thomas,
There are that dare, and I myself have ventur'd   40
To speak my mind of him : and indeed this day,
Sir (I may tell it you) I think I have
Incens'd the lords o' the council, that he is
(For so I know he is, they know he is)
A most arch-heretic, a pestilence
That does infect the land : with which they mov'd

Have broken with the king, who hath so far
Given ear to our complaint, of his great grace,
And princely care, foreseeing those fell mischiefs
Our reasons laid before him, hath commanded   50
To-morrow morning to the council-board
He be convented.   He's a rank weed, Sir Thomas,
And we must root him out.   From your affairs
I hinder you too long : good night, Sir Thomas.

Lov. Many good nights, my lord : I rest your servant.

Exeunt Gardiner and Page
Enter King and Suffolk

Hen. Charles, I will play no more to-night,
My mind's not on 't, you are too hard for me.

Suf. Sir, I did never win of you before.

Hen. But little, Charles,
Nor shall not, when my fancy's on my play.   60
Now, Lovell, from the queen what is the news ?

Lov. I could not personally deliver to her
What you commanded me, but by her woman
I sent your message, who return'd her thanks
In the great'st humbleness, and desir'd your highness
Most heartily to pray for her.

Hen.   What say'st thou, ha ?
To pray for her ? what, is she crying out ?

Lov. So said her woman, and that her sufferance made

Almost each pang a death.

Hen.   Alas, good lady !

Suf. God safely quit her of her burthen, and   70
  With gentle travail, to the gladding of
  Your highness with an heir !

Hen.   'Tis midnight, Charles,
  Prithee to bed, and in thy prayers remember
  The estate of my poor queen.   Leave me alone,
  For I must think of that which company
  Would not be friendly to.

Suf.   I wish your highness
  A quiet night, and my good mistress will
  Remember in my prayers.

Hen.   Charles, good night.   *Exit Suffolk*
                          Enter Sir Anthony Denny
  Well, sir, what follows ?

Den. Sir, I have brought my lord the archbishop,   80
  As you commanded me.

Hen.   Ha ? Canterbury ?

Den. Ay, my good lord.

Hen.   'Tis true : where is he, Denny ?

Den. He attends your highness' pleasure.

Hen.   Bring him to us.
                          Exit Denny

Lov. (*aside*) This is about that which the bishop spake.

I am happily come hither.

Re-enter Denny, with Cranmer

Hen. Avoid the gallery. (*Lovell seems to stay.*) Ha? I have
said.   Be gone.

What ?   *Exeunt Lovell and Denny*

Cra.   (*aside*) I am fearful : wherefore frowns he thus ?
'Tis his aspect of terror.   All's not well.

Hen. How now, my lord ? you do desire to know
Wherefore I sent for you.

Cra. (*kneeling*)   It is my duty   90
To attend your highness' pleasure.

Hen.   Pray you, arise,
My good and gracious Lord of Canterbury.
Come, you and I must walk a turn together ;
I have news to tell you.   Come, come, give me your
hand.
Ah, my good lord, I grieve at what I speak,
And am right sorry to repeat what follows.
I have, and most unwillingly, of late
Heard many grievous, I do say, my lord,
Grievous complaints of you ; which, being consider'd,
Have mov'd us and our council, that you shall   100
This morning come before us, where, I know,
You cannot with such freedom purge yourself,
But that, till further trial in those charges

Which will require your answer, you must take
Your patience to you, and be well contented
To make your house our Tower : you, a brother of us, †
It fits we thus proceed, or else no witness
Would come against you.

Cra. (*kneeling*)   I humbly thank your highness,
And am right glad to catch this good occasion
Most throughly to be winnow'd, where my chaff   110
And corn shall fly asunder.   For I know
There's none stands under more calumnious tongues
Than I myself, poor man.

Hen.   Stand up, good Canterbury ;
Thy truth, and thy integrity, is rooted
In us, thy friend.   Give me thy hand, stand up,
Prithee let's walk.   Now, by my holidame,
What manner of man are you ?   My lord, I look'd
You would have given me your petition, that
I should have ta'en some pains, to bring together
Yourself and your accusers, and to have heard you   120
Without indurance further.

Cra.   Most dread liege,
The good I stand on is my truth and honesty :
If they shall fail, I, with mine enemies,
Will triumph o'er my person, which I weigh not
Being of those virtues vacant.   I fear nothing

What can be said against me.

Hen.   Know you not
How your state stands i' the world, with the whole
    world ?
Your enemies are many, and not small ; their practices
Must bear the same proportion, and not ever
The justice and the truth o' the question carries   130
The due o' the verdict with it : at what ease
Might corrupt minds procure knaves as corrupt
To swear against you ?   Such things have been done.
You are potently oppos'd, and with a malice
Of as great size.   Ween you of better luck,
I mean, in perjur'd witness, than your master,
Whose minister you are, whiles here he liv'd
Upon this naughty earth ?   Go to, go to,
You take a precipice for no leap of danger,
And woo your own destruction.

Cra.   God, and your majesty,   140
Protect mine innocence, or I fall into
The trap is laid for me !

Hen.   Be of good cheer,
They shall no more prevail than we give way to :
Keep comfort to you, and this morning see
You do appear before them.   If they shall chance,
In charging you with matters, to commit you,

The best persuasions to the contrary
Fail not to use, and with what vehemency
The occasion shall instruct you.   If entreaties
Will render you no remedy, this ring   150
Deliver them, and your appeal to us
There make before them.   (*aside*) Look, the good
     man weeps !
He 's honest, on mine honour.   God's blest mother,
I swear he is true-hearted, and a soul
None better in my kingdom.—Get you gone,
And do as I have bid you.   (*exit Cranmer.*) He has
     strangled
His language in his tears.

       Enter Old Lady : Lovell following

Gen.   (*within*) Come back : what mean you ?

La. I 'll not come back, the tidings that I bring
Will make my boldness manners.   Now good angels
Fly o'er thy royal head, and shade thy person   160
Under their blessed wings !

Hen.   Now by thy looks
I guess thy message.   Is the queen deliver'd ?
Say ay, and of a boy.

La.   Ay, ay, my liege,
And of a lovely boy : the God of heaven
Both now and ever bless her ! 'tis a girl

Promises boys hereafter.   Sir, your queen
Desires your visitation, and to be
Acquainted with this stranger ; 'tis as like you
As cherry is to cherry.

Hen.   Lovell !

Lov.   Sir ?

Hen. Give her an hundred marks.   I 'll to the queen.   170

Exit

La. An hundred marks ?   By this light, I 'll ha' more.
An ordinary groom is for such payment.
I will have more, or scold it out of him.
Said I for this, the girl was like to him ?   I 'll
Have more, or else unsay 't ; and now, while 'tis hot,
I 'll put it to the issue.   *Exeunt*

SCENE II

Before the council-chamber

Pursuivants, Pages, &c. attending

Enter Cranmer, Archbishop of Canterbury

Cra. I hope I am not too late, and yet the gentleman
That was sent to me from the council pray'd me
To make great haste.   All fast ? what means this ?
Ho !

Who waits there? Sure, you know me?
Enter Keeper

Kee.   Yes, my lord:
But yet I cannot help you.

Cra. Why?
Enter Doctor Butts

Kee. Your grace must wait till you be call'd for.

Cra.   So.

Doc. (*aside*) This is a piece of malice: I am glad
I came this way so happily.   The king
Shall understand it presently.   *Exit*

Cra.   (*aside*) 'Tis Butts,   10
The king's physician: as he pass'd along,
How earnestly he cast his eyes upon me!
Pray heaven he sound not my disgrace: for certain,
This is of purpose laid by some that hate me,
(God turn their hearts, I never sought their malice)
To quench mine honour; they would shame to
     make me
Wait else at door, a fellow-councillor,
'Mong boys, grooms, and lackeys.   But their pleasures
Must be fulfill'd, and I attend with patience.
Enter the King and Butts at a window above

Doc. I'll show your grace the strangest sight,

Hen.   What's that, Butts?   20

Doc. I think your highness saw this many a day.

Hen. Body o' me, where is it ?

Doc.   There, my lord :
The high promotion of his grace of Canterbury,
Who holds his state at door 'mongst pursuivants,
Pages, and footboys.

Hen.   Ha ! 'tis he, indeed :
Is this the honour they do one another ?
'Tis well there 's one above 'em yet ; I had thought
They had parted so much honesty among 'em,
At least good manners, as not thus to suffer
A man of his place, and so near our favour,   30
To dance attendance on their lordships' pleasures,
And at the door too, like a post with packets.
By holy Mary, Butts, there 's knavery ;
Let 'em alone, and draw the curtain close :
We shall hear more anon.   *Exeunt*

SCENE III

The council-chamber

*A council-table brought in with chairs and stools, and
placed under the state*

*Enter Lord Chancellor, places himself at the upper end of the
table on the left hand ; a seat being left void above him, as*

for Canterbury's seat ; Duke of Suffolk, Duke of Norfolk,
Surrey, Lord Chamberlain, Gardiner, seat themselves in
order on each side.   Cromwell at lower end, as secretary.
Keeper at the door.

Ch. Speak to the business, master secretary :
      Why are we met in council ?

Cro.   Please your honours,
      The chief cause concerns his grace of Canterbury.

Gar. Has he had knowledge of it ?

Cro.   Yes.

Nor.   Who waits there ?

Kee. Without, my noble lords ?

Gar.   Yes.

Kee.   My lord archbishop ;
      And has done half an hour, to know your pleasures.

Ch. Let him come in.

Kee.   Your grace may enter now.

           Cranmer enters and approaches the council-table

Ch. My good lord archbishop, I 'm very sorry
      To sit here at this present, and behold
      That chair stand empty : but we all are men,   10
      In our own natures frail, and capable
      Of our flesh, few are angels ; out of which frailty
      And want of wisdom, you, that best should teach us,
      Have misdemean'd yourself, and not a little :

Toward the king first, then his laws, in filling
The whole realm, by your teaching and your chaplains
(For so we are inform'd) with new opinions,
Divers and dangerous ; which are heresies ;
And, not reform'd, may prove pernicious.

Gar. Which reformation must be sudden too,   20
My noble lords ; for those that tame wild horses
Pace 'em not in their hands to make 'em gentle,
But stop their mouths with stubborn bits and spur 'em,
Till they obey the manage.   If we suffer,
Out of our easiness and childish pity
To one man's honour, this contagious sickness,
Farewell all physic : and what follows then ?
Commotions, uproars, with a general taint
Of the whole state ; as of late days our neighbours,
The upper Germany, can dearly witness,   30
Yet freshly pitied in our memories.

Cra. My good lords ; hitherto, in all the progress
Both of my life and office, I have labour'd,
And with no little study, that my teaching
And the strong course of my authority
Might go one way, and safely ; and the end
Was ever to do well : nor is there living,
(I speak it with a single heart, my lords)
A man that more detests, more stirs against,

128

Both in his private conscience, and his place,   40
Defacers of a public peace, than I do.
Pray heaven the king may never find a heart
With less allegiance in it !   Men that make
Envy and crooked malice nourishment
Dare bite the best.   I do beseech your lordships,
That, in this case of justice, my accusers,
Be what they will, may stand forth face to face,
And freely urge against me.

Suf.   Nay, my lord,
That cannot be ; you are a councillor,
And, by that virtue, no man dare accuse you.   50

Gar. My lord, because we have business of more moment,
We will be short with you.   'Tis his highness'
    pleasure,
And our consent, for better trial of you,
From hence you be committed to the Tower,
Where, being but a private man again,
You shall know many dare accuse you boldly,
More than, I fear, you are provided for.

Cra. Ah, my good Lord of Winchester ; I thank you,
You are always my good friend, if your will pass,
I shall both find your lordship judge and juror,   60
You are so merciful.   I see your end,
'Tis my undoing.   Love and meekness, lord,

Become a churchman better than ambition :
Win straying souls with modesty again,
Cast none away.   That I shall clear myself,
Lay all the weight ye can upon my patience,
I make as little doubt as you do conscience
In doing daily wrongs.   I could say more,
But reverence to your calling makes me modest.

Gar. My lord, my lord, you are a sectary,   70
That's the plain truth ; your painted gloss discovers,
To men that understand you, words and weakness.

Cro. My Lord of Winchester, you are a little,
By your good favour, too sharp ; men so noble,
However faulty, yet should find respect
For what they have been : 'tis a cruelty
To load a falling man.

Gar.   Good master secretary,
I cry your honour mercy ; you may worst
Of all this table say so.

Cro.   Why, my lord ?

Gar. Do not I know you for a favourer   80
Of this new sect ? ye are not sound.

Cro.   Not sound ?

Gar. Not sound, I say.

Cro.   Would you were half so honest !
Men's prayers then would seek you, not their fears.

Gar. I shall remember this bold language.

Cro.   Do.
Remember your bold life too.

Ch.   This is too much ;
Forbear, for shame, my lords.

Gar.   I have done.

Cro.   And I.

Ch. Then thus for you, my lord, it stands agreed,
I take it, by all voices : that forthwith
You be convey'd to the Tower a prisoner ;
There to remain till the king's further pleasure   90
Be known unto us : are you all agreed, lords ?

All. We are.

Cra.   Is there no other way of mercy,
But I must needs to the Tower, my lords ?

Gar.   What other
Would you expect ? you are strangely troublesome :
Let some o' the guard be ready there.

                    Enter Guard

Cra.   For me ?
Must I go like a traitor thither ?

Gar.   Receive him,
And see him safe i' the Tower.

Cra.   Stay, good my lords,
I have a little yet to say.   Look there, my lords,

                    131

By virtue of that ring, I take my cause
Out of the gripes of cruel men, and give it   100
To a most noble judge, the king my master.

L.C. This is the king's ring.

Sur.   'Tis no counterfeit.

Suf. 'Tis the right ring, by heaven : I told ye all,
When we first put this dangerous stone a-rolling,
'Twould fall upon ourselves.

Nor.   Do you think, my lords,
The king will suffer but the little finger
Of this man to be vex'd ?

L.C.   'Tis now too certain :
How much more is his life in value with him ?
Would I were fairly out on 't !

Cro.   My mind gave me,
In seeking tales and informations   110
Against this man, whose honesty the devil
And his disciples only envy at,
Ye blew the fire that burns ye : now have at ye !

Enter King, frowning on them ; takes his seat

Gar. Dread sovereign, how much are we bound to heaven
In daily thanks, that gave us such a prince,
Not only good and wise, but most religious :
One that, in all obedience, makes the church
The chief aim of his honour, and, to strengthen

That holy duty, out of dear respect,
His royal self in judgement comes to hear   120
The cause betwixt her and this great offender.

Hen. You were ever good at sudden commendations,
Bishop of Winchester.   But know I come not
To hear such flattery now, and in my presence
They are too thin and bare to hide offences.
To me you cannot reach : you play the spaniel,
And think with wagging of your tongue to win me ;
But, whatsoe'er thou tak'st me for, I'm sure
Thou hast a cruel nature and a bloody.
     (*to Cranmer*) Good man, sit down.   Now let me
          see the proudest   130
He, that dares most, but wag his finger at thee :
By all that's holy, he had better starve
Than but once think this place becomes thee not.

Sur. May it please your grace,—

Hen.   No, sir, it does not please me ;
I had thought I had had men of some understanding
And wisdom of my council ; but I find none :
Was it discretion, lords, to let this man,
This good man (few of you deserve that title)
This honest man, wait like a lousy footboy
At chamber-door ? and one as great as you are ?   140
Why, what a shame was this !   Did my commission

Bid ye so far forget yourselves ?   I gave ye
Power as he was a councillor to try him,
Not as a groom : there's some of ye, I see,
More out of malice than integrity,
Would try him to the utmost, had ye mean,
Which ye shall never have while I live.

Ch.   Thus far,
My most dread sovereign, may it like your grace
To let my tongue excuse all.   What was purpos'd
Concerning his imprisonment, was rather   150
(If there be faith in men) meant for his trial,
And fair purgation to the world, than malice,
I'm sure, in me.

Hen.   Well, well, my lords, respect him,
Take him, and use him well ; he's worthy of it.
I will say thus much for him, if a prince
May be beholding to a subject, I
Am for his love and service so to him.
Make me no more ado, but all embrace him ;
Be friends, for shame, my lords !   My Lord of
          Canterbury,
I have a suit which you must not deny me ;   160
That is, a fair young maid that yet wants baptism,
You must be godfather, and answer for her.

Cra. The greatest monarch now alive may glory

In such an honour : how may I deserve it,
That am a poor and humble subject to you ?

Hen. Come, come, my lord, you 'ld spare your spoons :
        you shall have
    Two noble partners with you ; the old Duchess
    Of Norfolk, and Lady Marquess Dorset : will these
        please you ?
    Once more, my Lord of Winchester, I charge you,
    Embrace and love this man.

Gar.   With a true heart   170
    And brother-love I do it.

Cra.   And let heaven
    Witness how dear I hold this confirmation.

Hen. Good man, those joyful tears show thy true heart :
    The common voice, I see, is verified
    Of thee, which says thus : ' Do my Lord of Canter-
        bury
    A shrewd turn, and he is your friend for ever.'
    Come, lords, we trifle time away ; I long
    To have this young one made a Christian.
    As I have made ye one, lords, one remain :
    So I grow stronger, you more honour gain.   *Exeunt* 180

SCENE IV

The palace yard

Noise and tumult within.   Enter Porter and his Man

Por. You'll leave your noise anon, ye rascals : do you
    take the court for Paris-garden ? ye rude slaves,
    leave your gaping.

(One within) Good master porter, I belong to the larder.

Por. Belong to the gallows, and be hang'd, ye rogue !   Is
    this a place to roar in ?   Fetch me a dozen crab-tree
    staves, and strong ones : these are but switches to
    'em.   I'll scratch your heads : you must be seeing
    christenings ? do you look for ale and cakes here,
    you rude rascals ?

10

Man. Pray, sir, be patient, 'tis as much impossible,
    Unless we sweep 'em from the door with cannons,
    To scatter 'em, as 'tis to make 'em sleep
    On May-day morning, which will never be :
    We may as well push against Powle's as stir 'em.

Por. How got they in, and be hang'd ?

Man. Alas, I know not, how gets the tide in ?
    As much as one sound cudgel of four foot
    (You see the poor remainder) could distribute,
    I made no spare, sir.

Por.   You did nothing, sir.   20

Man. I am not Samson, nor Sir Guy, nor Colbrand,   †
       To mow 'em down before me : but if I spar'd any
       That had a head to hit, either young or old,
       He or she, cuckold or cuckold-maker,
       Let me ne'er hope to see a chine again,
       And that I would not for a cow, God save her !

(One within) Do you hear, master porter ?

Por. I shall be with you presently, good master puppy.
       Keep the door close, sirrah.

Man. What would you have me do ?   30

Por. What should you do, but knock 'em down by the
       dozens ? Is this Moorfields to muster in ? or have
       we some strange Indian with the great tool come to
       court, the women so besiege us ? Bless me, what a
       fry of fornication is at door ! On my Christian con-
       science, this one christening will beget a thousand ;
       here will be father, godfather, and all together.

Man. The spoons will be the bigger, sir. There is a
       fellow somewhat near the door, he should be a
       brazier by his face, for, o' my conscience, twenty   40
       of the dog-days now reign in 's nose ; all that stand
       about him are under the line, they need no other
       penance : that fire-drake did I hit three times on the
       head, and three times was his nose discharged against

me ; he stands there like a mortar-piece to blow us.
There was a haberdasher's wife of small wit near him,
that rail'd upon me till her pink'd porringer fell off
her head, for kindling such a combustion in the state.
I missed the meteor once, and hit that woman, who
cried out ' Clubs ! ' when I might see from far some   50
forty truncheoners draw to her succour, which were
the hope o' the Strand, where she was quarter'd ;
they fell on ; I made good my place ; at length they
came to the broomstaff to me, I defied 'em still, when
suddenly a file of boys behind 'em, loose shot, deliver'd such a shower of pebbles, that I was fain to
draw mine honour in, and let 'em win the work : the
devil was amongst 'em I think surely.

Por. These are the youths that thunder at a playhouse,
and fight for bitten apples, that no audience but the   60
tribulation of Tower-hill, or the limbs of Limehouse,   †
their dear brothers, are able to endure.   I have some
of 'em in Limbo Patrum, and there they are like to
dance these three days ; besides the running banquet
of two beadles, that is to come.

Enter Lord Chamberlain

L.C. Mercy o' me, what a multitude are here !
They grow still too ; from all parts they are coming,
As if we kept a fair here.   Where are these porters ?

These lazy knaves? Ye've made a fine hand,
   fellows!
There's a trim rabble let in: are all these   70
Your faithful friends o' the suburbs? We shall have
Great store of room, no doubt, left for the ladies,
When they pass back from the christening.

Por.   An't please your honour,
We are but men; and what so many may do,
Not being torn a-pieces, we have done:
An army cannot rule 'em.

L.C.   As I live,
If the king blame me for 't, I'll lay ye all
By the heels, and suddenly; and on your heads
Clap round fines for neglect: ye're lazy knaves,
And here ye lie baiting of bombards, when   80
Ye should do service. Hark! the trumpets sound,
They're come already from the christening;
Go, break among the press, and find a way out
To let the troop pass fairly, or I'll find
A Marshalsea shall hold ye play these two months.

Por. Make way there for the princess.

Man.   You great fellow,
Stand up close, or I'll make your head ache.

Por. You i' the camlet, get up o' the rail,
I'll peck you o'er the pales else.   *Exeunt*

SCENE V

The palace

Enter Trumpets, sounding; then two Aldermen, Lord Mayor, Garter, Cranmer, Duke of Norfolk with his marshal's staff, Duke of Suffolk, two Noblemen bearing great standing-bowls for the christening gifts; then four Noblemen bearing a canopy, under which the Duchess of Norfolk, godmother, bearing the child richly habited in a mantle, &c., train borne by a Lady; then follows the Marchioness Dorset, the other godmother, and Ladies. The troop pass once about the stage, and Garter speaks.

Gar. Heaven, from thy endless goodness, send prosperous
life, long, and ever happy, to the high and mighty
princess of England, Elizabeth !

Flourish.   Enter King and Guard

Cra. (*kneeling*) And to your royal grace, and the good
queen.
My noble partners and myself thus pray,
All comfort, joy in this most gracious lady,
Heaven ever laid up to make parents happy,
May hourly fall upon ye !

Hen.   Thank you, good lord archbishop :
What is her name ?

Cra.   Elizabeth.

Hen.   Stand up, lord.
                          The King kisses the child

With this kiss, take my blessing : God protect thee,   10
Into whose hand I give thy life.

Cra.   Amen.

Hen. My noble gossips, ye have been too prodigal :
I thank ye heartily ; so shall this lady,
When she has so much English.

Cra.   Let me speak, sir.
For heaven now bids me ; and the words I utter
Let none think flattery ; for they 'll find 'em truth.
This royal infant (heaven still move about her)
Though in her cradle, yet now promises
Upon this land a thousand thousand blessings,
Which time shall bring to ripeness : she shall be,   20
(But few now living can behold that goodness)
A pattern to all princes living with her,
And all that shall succeed : Saba was never
More covetous of wisdom, and fair virtue,
Than this pure soul shall be.   All princely graces,
That mould up such a mighty piece as this is,
With all the virtues that attend the good,
Shall still be doubled on her.   Truth shall nurse her,
Holy and heavenly thoughts still counsel her :

She shall be lov'd and fear'd.   Her own shall bless
    her ;   30
Her foes shake like a field of beaten corn,
And hang their heads with sorrow.   Good grows
    with her :
In her days every man shall eat in safety,
Under his own vine, what he plants ; and sing
The merry songs of peace to all his neighbours :
God shall be truly known, and those about her
From her shall read the perfect way of honour,
And by those claim their greatness, not by blood.
Nor shall this peace sleep with her ; but, as when
The bird of wonder dies, the maiden phœnix,   40
Her ashes new create another heir,
As great in admiration as herself.
So shall she leave her blessedness to one,
(When heaven shall call her from this cloud of
    darkness)
Who, from the sacred ashes of her honour,
Shall star-like rise, as great in fame as she was,
And so stand fix'd.   Peace, Plenty, Love, Truth,
    Terror,
That were the servants to this chosen infant,
Shall then be his, and like a vine grow to him ;
Wherever the bright sun of heaven shall shine,   50

His honour, and the greatness of his name,
Shall be, and make new nations.   He shall flourish,
And, like a mountain cedar, reach his branches
To all the plains about him.   Our children's children
Shall see this, and bless heaven.

Hen.   Thou speakest wonders.

Cra. She shall be, to the happiness of England,
An aged princess ; many days shall see her,
And yet no day without a deed to crown it.
Would I had known no more ! but she must die,
She must, the saints must have her ; yet a virgin,   60
A most unspotted lily, shall she pass
To the ground, and all the world shall mourn her.

Hen. O lord archbishop,
Thou hast made me now a man ! never, before
This happy child, did I get any thing.
This oracle of comfort has so pleas'd me,
That when I am in heaven I shall desire
To see what this child does, and praise my Maker.
I thank ye all.   To you, my good lord mayor,
And your good brethren, I am much beholding :   70
I have receiv'd much honour by your presence,
And ye shall find me thankful.   Lead the way, lords,
Ye must all see the queen, and she must thank ye,
She will be sick else.   This day, no man think

Has business at his house ; for all shall stay :
This little one shall make it holiday.   *Exeunt*

THE EPILOGUE

'Tis ten to one this play can never please
All that are here : some come to take their ease,
And sleep an act or two ; but those, we fear,
We 've frighted with our trumpets ; so, 'tis clear,
They 'll say 'tis naught.   Others to hear the city
Abus'd extremely, and to cry ' That 's witty ! '
Which we have not done neither ; that I fear
All the expected good we 're like to hear
For this play at this time, is only in
The merciful construction of good women ;   10
For such a one we show'd 'em : if they smile,
And say 'twill do, I know, within a while
All the best men are ours ; for 'tis ill hap,
If they hold, when their ladies bid 'em clap.

Notes

THERE is a considerable number of passages in the play which present at least a momentary (and most readers will feel an un-Shakespearean) difficulty, not from the use of unusual words, nor from any involution of thought, but rather from tricks of syntax. It would, I think, be wearisome to have all these annotated, and they can hardly be glossed. I hope that the inclusion of the 'key-word' or 'key-phrase' in the Glossary will suffice to illuminate most of them. For example, in II. iv. 97-99, so soon as one sees that *your wrong* means 'the wrong you do me,' it becomes plain that the whole sentence means 'When he sees that I am clear of your charge against me he sees that I am not unwounded by (*i.e.* not free from, in another sense) the wrong you do me by making the charge.'

Prol. 25, 26. One feels that, in the interests of rhyme, we should either read *See before ye* for *Think ye see*, or *history* for *noble story*.

I. i. 7. *vale of Andren*; the scene of 'The Field of the Cloth of Gold.'

I. i. 38. *Bevis*; one of the Paladins, Bevis of Southampton.

I. i. 45-47. This is Theobald's division of speeches. F begins Buckingham's speech with *All was royal* and ends it with *together*. This opening is awkward; but the conclusion avoids the difficulty of *as you guess* as addressed to one who is not guessing at all, but reporting from personal observation.

I. i. 78. *his own letter . . . papers*; Pope's explanation is: "His own letter, by his own single authority, and without the concurrence of the council, must fetch him in whom he papers down" (*i.e.* registers). This seems clearly right down to the last four words of the text, but there the ellipse of *whom* is difficult. If we are to emend, the least dislocating suggestion is perhaps *fetch in whom he.*

I. i. 85. *What did this vanity* . . .; an obscure phrase. I do not think it amounts to much more than ' What did this folly achieve except to produce a poor result,' but it is a cumbrous way of saying it.

I. i. 90. *storm*; Holinshed records a 'hideous storme' which broke out and led to gloomy prognostications.

I. i. 111. *where 'twill not extend . . . dart it*; the picture seems to be of a weapon, whose range, as normally used in the hand, proves inadequate, suddenly used as a missile.

I. i. 152. *Whom from the flow of gall* . . .; i.e. ' I am not saying this merely because I am angry.'

I. i. 176. *Charles the emperor*; Charles V of Germany, Queen Katharine's nephew.

I. i. 204-6. *I am sorry . . . present*; Johnson explained, " I am sorry to be present and an eye-witness of your loss of liberty."

I. ii. 120. *ravish'd listening*; it is tempting to follow Pope and transpose the words.

I. ii. 147. *Henton*; this clearly should be *Hopkins*, as the monk is called in Holinshed; it is moderately clear that the error comes from a hurried glance at Holinshed, who writes, " Nicholas Hopkins, a monke of an house of Chartreux order beside Bristow called Henton," the ' called Henton ' being taken with the ' monke ' not the ' house.'

I. iii. 32. *understand*; this may mean no more than ' have their wits,' but I cannot help feeling that there is a pun ; ' they will stand on honest English legs again.' Cf. *Twelfth Night*, III. i. 90. (But admittedly the pun does not bear thinking out.)

I. iii. 34. *wee*; the later Folios read *wear*, an emendation as easy as unauthoritative. The conjecture that *wee* equals *oui* is hardly plausible. It is just worth nothing that in F there is a double space between the *o* of *privilegio* and the *w* of *wee*, as though a letter had dropped out. There is clearly some corruption. Just possibly *swet*.

I. iv. 6. *first*; this word is hardly satisfactory; but the conjectures are even less so. Perhaps Guildford, having addressed the ladies in l. 1, here turns to the men with *As, sirs*.

II. i. 29. *either pitied . . . forgotten*; Malone explains as meaning 'either produced (ineffectual) pity or no effect at all.'

II. ii. 61. *(S.D.)*; a very clear instance of the use of the rear-stage and its curtains.

II. iii. 14. *that quarrel, fortune, do divorce*; does *quarrel* mean 'quarreller,' as Johnson thought, or the arrow (of a crossbow)? If the second, Lettsom's conjecture is tempting, *fortune's quarrel* (then taking *if that*='if'). Either will make fair sense, but *quarrel* may be corrupt: and the F punctuation is a trifle suspicious, *if that quarrell. Fortune, do . . .*

II. iii. 89. *forty pence*; there is an odd little point here which may have some significance with regard to the problem of authorship. Forty pence was an attorney's fee, and (as here) a common phrase for a small bet ('bet you a bob'); but, whereas Beaumont and Fletcher use the phrase, Shakespeare, as it happens, never does, but always the equivalent, 'ten groats.'

II. iv. 61. *That longer you desire the court*; there seems no need for the emendation of *desire*; the phrase is not easy, but Malone's explanation seems adequate, "you desire to protract the business of the court."

III. i. 23. *All hoods make not monks*; the old proverb, *Cucullus non facit monachum.*

III. ii. 64-66. There are two problems; does Suffolk mean that Cranmer has returned steadfast in his opinions, or that he has in effect returned; by sending a report of his opinions in front of him? And is *colleges* genitive plural or accusative?

III. ii. 192. *that am, have, and will be*; the pother that this line has caused (over twenty emendations have been suggested) illustrates the perils of reading Shakespeare with a text-book of grammar instead of with imagination. Wolsey is not writing a school exercise, but making a speech under strong emotion, and his meaning is as clear as his syntax is faulty. He is about to say that he is, has been, and will always be, the king's; the parenthesis breaks the run of the sentence, and the construction is never picked up again, though the sense is.

III. ii. 280-82. Larks were frightened and kept quiet till netted by waving a piece of scarlet cloth.

IV. i. 11. *Pageants*; the pageant was a ' spectacle ' (a tableau or the like) mounted on a movable platform so that it could be drawn in a procession, exactly like one of the disguised cars with its freight in a continental carnival's battle of flowers or in the Lord Mayor's Show.

IV. ii. 58. *twins of learning*; Wolsey's College, Ipswich, and Christ Church, Oxford.

V. i. 106. *you, a brother of us*; i.e. one of the Council.

V. iv. 21. *Sir Guy, nor Colbrand*; it is related in the romances that Sir Guy of Warwick killed a Danish giant named Colbrand.

V. iv. 61. *tribulation . . . Limehouse*; clearly a topical allusion, to which we have lost the key, though various attempts have been made to cut one.

Glossary

MANY words and phrases in Shakespeare require glossing, not because they are in themselves unfamiliar, but for the opposite reason, that Shakespeare uses in their Elizabethan and unfamiliar sense a large number of words which seem so familiar that there is no incentive to look for them in the glossary. It is hoped that a glossary arranged as below will make it easy to see at a glance what words and phrases in any particular scene require elucidation. A number of phrases are glossed by what seems to be, in their context, the modern equivalent rather than by lexicographical glosses on the words which compose them.

The Prologue

line
3 SAD, sober
  WORKING, working on the emotions

line
11 PASS, pass muster with
16 GUARDED, trimmed
25 SAD, sober

Act First

SCENE I

2 SAW, *sc.* each other
3 ADMIRER OF, wonderer at
10 AS, as though
19 CLINQUANT, glittering
25 PRIDE, ostentatious finery
26 PAINTING, rouging
30 IN EYE, under observation
33 CENSURE, comparative judgment
39 BELONG TO WORSHIP, am of noble rank

39 AFFECT HONESTY, love truth
40 TRACT, course of action
44 OFFICE, officials
48 PROMISES NO ELEMENT, does not look likely to share
54 FIERCE, extravagant
55 KEECH, lump of fat (*W.* was a butcher's son)
59 WHOSE, of which
60 CHALKS, marks out

15 *l*

KING HENRY VIII

Act I Sc. i—*continued*

line
- 73 FRENCH GOING OUT, expedition to France
- 88 NOT VALUES, is not worth (*ne vaux pas*)
- 91 NOT CONSULTING, independently
- 93 ABODED, foreboded
- 95 FLAW'D THE LEAGUE, broken the treaty
  - ATTACH'D, confiscated
- 100 LIKE IT, if it please
- 108 IN, in the shape of
- 115 SURVEYOR, steward of the household
- 122 BEGGAR'S BOOK, beggarly scholar
- 124 APPLIANCE ONLY, sole remedy

line
- 128 BORES, cheats
- 130 QUESTION, debate
- 139 DIFFERENCE IN NO PERSONS, no distinction of persons
- 144 MOUNTS, causes to mount
- 150 TOP-PROUD, proud in the extreme
- 153 MOTIONS, conviction
- 164 SUGGESTS, prompts
- 167 WRENCHING, rinsing
- 169 COMBINATION, agreement
- 188 COLOUR, pretext
- 204 PRACTICE, trickery
- 223 SPANN'D, come to end of its span

SCENE II

- 2 LEVEL, line of fire
- 24 PUTTER ON, instigator
- 26 SOIL, soiling
- 33 SPINSTERS, spinners
  - CARDERS, wool-carders
  - FULLERS, dry-cleaners
- 42 PERTAINS, which pertains
  - FRONT BUT IN THAT FILE, am front-rank man of a file
- 67 PRIMER, most pressing
- 70 NOT PASS'D ME, did not pass my lips
- 75 BRAKE, thicket
- 78 COPE, run up against
- 90 EXAMPLE, precedent

- 96 LOP, smaller twigs
- 105 HARDLY CONCEIVE, think hardly
- 110 IN, into
- 112 BOUND, indebted
- 114 OUT OF, outside
- 127 PRACTICES, sharp-practices
- 131 OUT OF, in the matter of
- 145 OUR FAIL, failure of our direct line
- 152 ROSE, *i.e.* the Red Rose (a manor of Buckingham's)
- 167 WITH DEMURE CONFIDENCE, confiding discretely
- 209 PERIOD, full-stop
- 210 ATTACH'D, arrested

SCENE III

line
2 MYSTERIES, fantasticalities
7 FIT, trick
8 DIRECTLY, on the spot
10 PEPIN OR CLOTHARIUS, ancient kings of France
12 SPAVIN, SPRINGHALT, diseases of horses, the first producing a halting, the second a jerky, gait
30 TALL, long

line
31 BLISTER'D, puffed
  TYPES, signs
40 SPEEDING, successful
41 FELLOW, equal
45 PLAIN-SONG, melody (*i.e.* without supporting harmony)
48 COLT'S TOOTH, *met. for* youth
67 COMPTROLLERS, masters of ceremonies

SCENE IV

(1 stage-directions) STATE, canopy
12 RUNNING BANQUET, slight collation

33 CURE, charge (*as in 'cure of souls'*)
34 LET ME ALONE, ' trust me '

Act Second

SCENE I

54 TIPSTAVES, ushers (with staves tipped with metal)
74 ONLY BITTER, the only bitterness
99 FURNITURE, furnishings

100 PERSON, rank
129 RUB, obstacle
149 HELD NOT, did not continue

SCENE II

2 RIDDEN, trained
3 FURNISH'D, equipped
21 TURNS WHAT HE LIST, manages things as he likes
49 PITCH, height
69 ESTATE, state
74 QUIET, soother

99 CONCLAVE, College of Cardinals
106 UNPARTIAL, impartial
112 SCHOLARS ALLOW'D, scholars of repute
128 FOREIGN, exiled
135 GRIP'D, grappled
141 ABLE, in full vigour

KING HENRY VIII

SCENE III

line
21 PERK'D UP, finely dressed,
      pranked up
22 CONTENT, contentment
23 HAVING, possession
31 MINCING, prudery
32 CHEVERIL, kid-leather, 'elastic'
36 THREE-PENCE BOW'D, bent 3d. bit
40 PLUCK OFF A LITTLE, come down
      a step (*i.e. duchess to countess*)
47 EMBALLING, probably a pun on

line
(*a*) physical intercourse, (*b*) de-
      coration with ball as symbol of
      royalty
74 CONCEIT, estimate
85 SUIT OF, suing for
87 COMPELL'D, forced upon one
93 YOUR THEME, you as my subject
97 MO, more (*Eliz. plur.*)
103 SALUTE, quickens
      FAINTS ME, causes me faintness

SCENE IV

(1 stage-directions) SENNET, elabor-
      ate flourish on trumpets
31 TO HIM DERIV'D, drawn upon
      him
48 BY, for
99 YOUR WRONG, the wrong you do
      me
154 TOUCH, injury

156 ARE NOT TO BE TAUGHT, need not
      be informed
165 SPEAK, give witness in favour of
      TO, on
191 OR . . . OR, either . . . or
198 HULLING, drifting
207 REEK, sweat

Act Third

SCENE I

17 PRESENCE, presence-chamber
77 FIT, *either* spasm (*i.e. brief
      period*), *or, perhaps*, canto or
      section of a poem
85 SO DESPERATE TO BE, so foolish as
      to be

116 HABITS, clothes
130 FONDNESS, foolishness
      SUPERSTITIOUS, idolatrously de-
      voted

SCENE II

line		line	
13	OUT OF, apart from	274	MATE, rival
29	PRACTICES, manœuvres	295	SACRING BELL, bell rung at elevation of the Host
48	COASTS AND HEDGES, proceeds circuitously	339	LEGATIVE, of a legate
101	HARD-RUL'D, hard to guide	340	PRÆMUNIRE, a writ directing the sheriff to arrest one who maintained the papal supremacy against the ecclesiastic supremacy of the Crown
105	FRET, chafe to breaking-point		
142	ILL HUSBAND, bad manager		
171	FILED, marched evenly with		
214	CROSS DEVIL, imp of perversity		
261	HIS, *objective* (not *subjective*) genitive		

Act Fourth

SCENE I

The Order of the Coronation

line		line	
5	GARTER, Garter King-of-Arms, the chief herald of the College of Arms	6	ESSES, *i.e.* SS (a chain of office with links in form of the letter S)
		8	IN HER HAIR, with her hair down
68	OPPOSING, showing	78	RAMS, battering-rams
73	SHROUDS, standing rigging which supports the mast laterally		

SCENE II

line		line	
34	STOMACH, pride	94	MUSIC, band of musicians
35	SUGGESTION, false representations		LEAVE, cease
36	TIED, held down	145	CARRIAGE, behaviour

Act Fifth

SCENE I

line

7 PRIMERO, gambling card game

36 GAP AND TRADE, beaten path ('*trade*' is a variant of '*tread*')

60 FANCY, mind

68 SUFFERANCE, suffering

line

86 AVOID, depart from

121 INDURANCE FURTHER, imprisonment besides

135 WEEN YOU OF, do you expect?

139 FOR, to be

SCENE II

10 PRESENTLY, immediately

24 PURSUIVANTS, heralds' attendants

SCENE III

11 CAPABLE OF OUR FLESH, susceptible to 'the flesh'

22 IN THEIR HANDS, on a long rein

24 MANAGE, '*manège*,' the indications (the 'aids') of the rider

70 SECTARY. See ll. 80, 81

71 PAINTED GLOSS DISCOVERS, painted veneer (*when removed*) discloses

146 MEANS, means

SCENE IV

2 PARIS-GARDEN, a well-known bear-garden on the Bank-side

15 POWLE's, St Paul's

24 CUCKOLD, husband of unfaithful wife

32 MOORFIELDS, place of exercise of train-bands

41 DOG-DAYS, hottest days of year

43 FIRE-DRAKE, fiery dragon

45 MORTAR-PIECE, small cannon

47 PINK'D PORRINGER, small round pierced toque

49 METEOR, *i.e. the 'fire-drake' of* l. 43

Act V   Sc. iv—*continued*

line
50 CLUBS, the cry to the prentices to share in or quell a fight

54 TO THE BROOMSTAFF, to close quarters

63 LIMBO PATRUM (*properly the place where the just after death await Christ's coming; sometimes used vaguely for Hell, and here prison*)

71 THE SUBURBS, *the traditional*

line
situation of disorderly houses and residence of the rabble in general

80 BAITING OF BOMBARDS, crowding round a large drinking-vessel like dogs at a bear-baiting

85 MARSHALSEA, prison

88 CAMLET, rough material

89 PECK, pitch
PALES, paling

SCENE V

12 GOSSIPS, godparents

23 SABA, the Queen of Sheba

Epilogue

14 HOLD, hold back